The HEOGAN Story

The HEOGAN Story

A link with the past

by

James H. Tulloch

2013

First published in United Kingdom in 2013
by James H. Tulloch, Bressay, Shetland.

A catalogue record for this book is available from the British Library.

ISBN 978-0-9575501-0-0

Printed by
The Shetland Times Ltd.,
Gremista, Lerwick,
Shetland ZE1 0PX.

This book is dedicated to the people, past and present, who have worked at Heogan over the years.

Contents

FOREWORD

THE fish meal factory at Heogan is still in operation, 130 years after it was first established. There are few businesses in Shetland with such a long and successful history. Of course, the factory has changed out of all recognition, with new piers, machinery and buildings. But it is still doing what it was set up to do all those years ago – to produce fish meal and oil from those parts of fish that cannot be used for human consumption.

Someone needed to write the history of this remarkable company and there is no one more able to do so than Hebbie Tulloch who was the Manager at Heogan for so many years.

I have known Hebbie for a long time. When we first met we argued about the price of sand eels. I was working for the Fishermens Association and Hebbie was Manager of the factory. Much later Hebbie and I became business partners in Bressay Salmon. Above all we are good friends.

This is not a dry account of fish meal production. Instead it is very readable and personal account by Hebbie of his time with the company and the many different people who worked at Heogan and landed fish at Heogan. It is above all else a story about the people involved – the fishermen, the factory workers and the wider community of Bressay and Shetland. The hundreds of Shetlanders who have landed fish to Heogan or have worked there will obviously find this book interesting. It will, however, also interest a wider audience because this is also a book about working life in the Shetland fishing industry. The ups and downs of the business, the hard work and ingenuity of all involved and the endless good humour are all described in Hebbie's easy writing style.

I feel greatly privileged to have been asked to write this review. As the Chairman of Shetland Fish Products (the company which now owns and operates Heogan) I am conscious that we have a unique heritage of 130 years of producing fish meal on this site. In this book Hebbie has recorded much of this heritage in a very engaging and readable way.

John Goodlad

ACKNOWLEDGEMENTS

MY grateful thanks and appreciation goes to many people who have given help and encouragement in producing this book.

First and foremost to my Norwegian friend Inge Kolltveit who gave me the initial nudge when he said: "You *must* write a book about what you know from the factory, no one else can do it."

To my two sons Dag and Rune who have been there with support and encouragement when I felt like giving up, and for their guidance in getting to grips with my computer.

Special thanks go to Linda Sutherland for her sound advice and liberal use of her red pen throughout the various stages of writing the manuscript. To Hazel Tulloch for proof reading and advising on specific points in the manuscript, and for her help in sorting out the photographs.

To Harry Tulloch for making available company records which have been so valuable in compiling the story.

Perhaps my severest critic has been John Scott of Gardie who, when asked to give an honest evaluation, read the manuscript at the eleventh hour. I am grateful for his frank and useful comments though it gave me much extra work.

My thanks also go to a host of individuals who have given information and made available photographs from their private collections.

To John Coutts and Robert Johnston who granted permission to use some of their professional photographs and to Martin Smith for his much appreciated photographs of the sand eel fleet.

Thanks also to Stella Sutherland, Marjory Thompson and Jock Johnston, for their contribution to early history; to Shetland Museum and Archives, and Bressay Heritage Centre, for information supplied from their records.

To Magnus Shearer, who supplied photographs and gave information relating to their family business, J & M Shearer.

To Sigfinn and Petter Bartz-Johannessen in Bergen for granting permission to use photographs and information in the HBP 50th anniversary book 'In the beginning was the herring', by Fritjof Sælen.

My special thanks go to the present day Directors of SFP in Bressay for making available up-dated information relating to the past 22 years at

Heogan, and for their generous financial contribution towards publishing 'The Heogan Story'.

And last but not least my grateful thanks go to my wife Bjarnhild, for her help, support and understanding, not only in the writing of this book, but in everything that I have done during our 47 years of marriage.

INTRODUCTION

IT WAS with mixed feelings that I drove home from work on 30th June, 1986. The temporary job which began in May 1955 had come to an end. My work at the factory had been a great experience and had become a way of life. Twenty two years as factory manager had, however, carried a good measure of stress, and the time had come to move on.

This book is the history of how a factory was built at Heogan on Bressay 130 years ago and of the changes and developments from the days of primitive production methods to the modern well equipped factory of today. It is based on research and hearsay with contributions from men who have worked at Heogan in bygone years. Reference is made to the boom time of the Shetlands herring fishery with numerous herring curing stations dotted around the islands.

In addition to recording the history of the Heogan factory this book is an account of my working life and of the people I met at Heogan, Fraserburgh, Norway and Barra during the years 1955 to 1987. It was never intended to be a record of Shetlands fishing industry. I have, however, attempted to show the economic importance of fishing to the local economy, and how the factory at Heogan has served and worked hand in hand with the industry.

A follow up shows something of my involvement in salmon farming. The final chapter cover the period 1990 up to the present day with some thought as to what the future may hold for the factory.

To write in detail about everyone who has worked at Heogan would be impossible; a comprehensive list of employees is, however, shown in the appendix. Some peerie stories, as they came to mind, are added for interest and are not intended to cause offence to any individual or their families.

Many of my former workmates have passed on, but I have omitted the term 'late' as it would be too repetitive. Looking back, it would be easier to record the names of Bressay men who have never worked at Heogan than those who have. But men from all over Shetland, and far beyond, have found employment at the factory. The factory has been, and remains a valuable and necessary part of Shetland's fishing industry. It has been of great importance to Bressay, providing the only real source of employment on the island since the boom days of the herring curers.

Development at Heogan has continued into a new millennium. Sadly, with the recent downturn in industrial fishing, raw material is now in short supply. Nevertheless, the Heogan factory is still a very important part of the local industry, providing an outlet for offal and rejected fish.

There are some gaps in the story where records are non-existent. With lack of group photographs, some photos of individuals who have worked at Heogan are shown. As a substitute, stills have been reproduced from 8mm movie film. Every effort has been made to portray a true account of *The Heogan Story*. For any mistakes, misinterpretations or omissions I offer my sincere apologies.

James H. Tulloch

1

My Path to Heogan

I WAS BORN at Wart Cottage Bressay on 26th March1935. My parents and grandparents were all born on the island. Father had been very ill in 1928, and following a prolonged stay in an Edinburgh hospital suffered a severe weakness in his left leg. As a result he failed the medical examination for military service. During the war years his work in the construction industry included building reinforced concrete air raid shelters at schools and other locations in Shetland.

Father took tenancy of the East Ham croft in 1946, and we moved into the croft house in 1947. His already poor health suffered as a result of the extra workload and Mother became the breadwinner in a never ending struggle with her knitting needles. Crofting was a way of life, with little financial reward.

Life on Bressay in the 1930s bore little resemblance to that of today. The laird, Norman Cameron, owned the only car on the island and tractors were unheard of. Lowrie Irvine operated a local bus service. Bressay women did their shopping on a particular day of the week. Lerwick day for the south end was always on Fridays, and Lowrie's bus service was a great asset. Apart from the limited bus service, people simply walked.

A common sight at the Mail pier was a row of colourful wheel barrows, lined up awaiting the shoppers return. Every household owned a 'Lerwick borrow'. The MV *Brenda*, a former German ships lifeboat from World War 1 was Bressay's ferry boat, providing not only a service from the Mail pier but also to Heogan, a remote community on the island. The *Brenda* made a weekly run to a wooden jetty at the factory for the benefit of Heogan shoppers.

In the 1930s a proper road to Heogan was lacking. Father told me that when he worked at Heogan at that time, he had to go through eight gates on the track leading from Maryfield to Heogan.

My so-called education was ten years at Bressay Public School. I left school in May 1950 lacking a secondary education. On leaving school at fifteen, I was determined to find work and stand on my own feet. I have always loved the sea and had an ambition to become a seaman or fisherman, but there was one big problem. I got violently seasick in any kind of boat.

During the 1950s Shetland's economy was at low ebb, with little work opportunity. There was of course the factory at Heogan, where my father had worked in the 1930s. He had many stories to tell from that time, but the thought of work in a factory did not appeal to me.

I considered emigration to New Zealand, where we had close relatives, having received two offers of employment from Bressay exiles. Mother was not happy at the prospect. Her brother and sister had emigrated 30 years earlier and she had not seen them since. If I went to New Zealand, she would never see me again, she said. In the end I gave up the argument and got work at Sumburgh farm – a dairy farm at the time. After three months at Sumburgh I moved to Orkney, working on a farm there for the next four and a half years.

By March 1955 I was finding farm work hard going, following a mysterious illness during the previous winter. I returned home with the intention of doing my stint of National Service. While awaiting call up papers, I took whatever work was available. One short term job was maintenance of the local by-roads. My workmates were Robbie Gifford and Robbie Sinclair. Robbie Gifford had worked at the Aith Voe factory in his young days. He lived at Kirkabister and walked the five miles to work each day.

The local herring fishery would commence in early May, and Robbie Sinclair would be going back to Heogan to work as a plant operator for the season. His work as drier man was 'money for old rope' he said, it entailed only adjusting a few valves. Robbie strongly advised me to apply for a job in the factory. With his persuasion and enthusiasm, I decided to give it a go.

On 17ᵗʰ May 1955 I headed for Heogan, hoping to get an interview. Father volunteered to accompany me. Our transport to Heogan was on his 6 h.p. Iron Horse tractor, which he had converted to a four wheeler with a top speed of 5 miles/hour.

We saw the factory launch approaching, driven by Andrew White, the assistant manager. When I told him that I was looking for work, he had only one question: "Can you start tomorrow night?"

Jamie Tulloch, author's father, on converted tractor, 1955.

It was agreed that the job would be temporary, while awaiting my call up papers for National Service. Little did I realise that Heogan would be my workplace for the next 31 years.

Andrew White, Bressay,
Manager: Laurence Anderson

2

EARLY HISTORY

DUTCH fishermen had been fishing successfully for herring in the North Sea for some 200 years before a Shetland herring fishery was established. Early attempts at a local level began about 1830. Fishing boats in use at the time were 'sixerns'. These small open boats had a very limited carrying capacity. The fishery got off to a slow start and during the 1830's, less than 3,000 barrels of salt herring were packed annually. Unpredicted storms at sea had a disastrous effect on the open boats, fishing up to forty miles off shore. In July 1832 an unexpected gale resulted in the loss of 31 boats and 105 men. Many more would have perished that day had it not been for the presence of the Dutch fleet which came to their rescue. Several more disasters followed with a devastating loss of human life. The disaster of 1842, with a loss of the fleet's nets, led to the collapse of the Shetland Bank. It put paid to the early herring fishery.

Real development finally began in the 1880's, when curing stations were set up at numerous locations throughout the islands. Shetland's herring fishery probably reached its peak about 1905, when over one million barrels of salt herring were exported. That year, a combination of Scottish, English, and Shetland boats landed their catch in Shetland. The fleet totalled 1,700 vessels and 12,500 fishermen. Shetland's share numbered 300 boats and 2,000 fishermen.

On 2nd September 1883 the following article was published in The Shetland Times:

> *"It is reported that Messrs Golding & Co are to start a manure factory on the island of Bressay. The primary arrangement has been completed. Hitherto the fishermen*

and fish curers have been unable to get all their offal sold and consequently the greater part of it has been thrown into the sea.

A manufacture for (the same) purpose has been started at Baltasound and has been in operation with very successful results for some weeks"

The original factory.   Bressay Heritage Centre

With an abundance of herring offal going to waste and polluting Lerwick harbour, it was imperative to find a use for this waste product. The fish reduction plant at Heogan, Bressay was to solve the problem.

Situated within Lerwick harbour, the site was at the outset ideal for a fish offal reduction plant. Fresh water was at hand and could be supplemented from a nearby loch during dry weather. A storage tank with retaining walls of mass concrete was built and referred to as 'The Dam'. It is still in use today. Early requirements were to build a pier and to provide accommodation for the workers. Fish storage bins were constructed partially below ground level and would thereafter be referred to as 'The Pits'.

When the process building complete with machinery and a 60 foot high brick chimney for the coal fired boiler was erected, the factory became operational.

The building project was labour intensive and would have taken some time. It is unclear exactly when production started but unlikely that it could have been before 1885. Records found indicate that the factory was operational by 1888.

During the early 1900s, three reduction plants were in operation in Shetland; namely Baltasound, Heogan and Aiths Voe. Today there is only three in the whole of the UK.

On 28th July 1883, 'Ground for let at Aiths Voe Bressay' was advertised in The Shetland Times. What is known is that the site's original use was as a herring curing station but no records have been found regarding the original development. Records in the Gardie papers show that in 1912 and again in 1926 the site was leased to J M Davidson.

The Aiths Voe factory was even more remote than Heogan. Many of the Bressay men who worked there lived in bothy accommodation during the week. One exception was Robbie Gifford who did the daily walk from Kirkabister, a round trip of more than ten miles.

George Sutherland of Gunnista was interviewed by Bressay Heritage Centre in October 1991. He remembered the factory in use, and recalled that the foreshore in the Voe was polluted by effluent.

The process at both Bressay factories was similar, but at Aiths Voe women were employed to repair burst bags. Women were never employed in that capacity at Heogan. The photo of the Aiths Voe factory workers in the late 1920s is courtesy of Adam Gifford. His father, Adam, is on the picture.

Geordie Sutherland ready for the peat hill.

*Heogan factory, 1906. From left – back: Robert Smith, James Bolt, Laurence White,
James J. Smith, Davie White (father of Andrew White). Middle: Laurence Linklater,
Geordie Gifford, Dick Emery (married to Geordie Gifford's daughter, Mary Ann),
Jock Emery, ? Emery, Jimmy Cooper, Hunter Nelson. Front: small Emery boy,
Arthur Cooper.   Marjorie Thomson*

Father had told me that the company's closure was linked to
investment in a new offal conveying system. The factory manager was
Andy Dalziel, a Bressay man who later emmigrated to New Zealand. John
Scott of Gardie confirms that the factory closed in 1938 for economic
reasons.

Manson's Almanac of 1908 lists fish curers operating throughout
Shetland. It states:

> *"It is impossible to say for sure how many curers are
> operating in Baltasound and Uyeasound. Those who have
> sites are listed."*

Aiths Voe workers in the 1930s. From left – back: unknown, W. Eunson, unknown, Adam Gifford, H. MacDonald, R. Eunson. Front: unknown, unknown, unknown, G. Smith, G. Sulloch, unknown, C. Stove, ? Johnson. It is possible the unknown men were fronm Unst as several Unst men were at Heogan and at the Aith factory.

Adam Gifford

This is a copy of the list:

Aith's Voe, Cunningsburgh	1
Baltasound	53
Bressay	9
Boddam	1
Burra Isle	2
Hammers Voe	2
Hillswick	2
Hoswick	11
Lerwick	41
Levenwick	2
North Roe	1
Scalloway	10
Skerries	1
Snarra Ness	1
Sumburgh	1
Uyeasound	4
Walls	3
West Sandwick	1
Whalsay	1
Whalfirth	1
Total	148

The 1908 Almanac also gives a list of (First-Class) Shetland fishing boats, with a keel length ranging from 40-60 feet and a few in excess of 70ft. The largest boat listed is SS *Dolphin* (LK564) shown as 95ft keel and 31 tons. This boat and several others were registered under the Merchant Shipping Act. The total number of boats listed is 265.

In the early years of the twentieth century, fifty fish curers were dotted along Lerwick's northern shore from Mitchell's point to Gremista and on Bressay from Heogan to Ham. Each curing yard had its own wooden pier and, to avoid confusion, had the station number displayed thereon. The skipper of a boat selling his catch was given the number of the appropriate station.

The station piers were constructed by driving disused railway beams into the sea bed with iron beams braced diagonally for strength. Heavy timber beams were used to support the top deck. A horizontal tide stringer, just above high water mark, acted as a fender and added strength to the structure. The discharge area had vertical timber fendering. Small gauge railway lines ran from the discharge point to the curing station where fishermen delivered their catch into the 'farlins' – wooden troughs. Delivery was by basket, four baskets to the cran.

Driftnet fishermen had a hard life, bearing little resemblance to that of today. At times, they worked almost day and night with little sleep during the herring season. Some stations were well back from the water front, and one in particular was on a steep incline, making it a very unpopular delivery point for the fishermen.

The Heogan pier was of similar design to those described above. Its purpose was to facilitate the intake of offal and dispatch of the finished products. Offal was collected from the fish curers in wooden barrels, which were headed up for transport by flit boats. On arrival at the pier, the barrels were placed on a bogie and propelled manually to the pits via a small gauge railway. With its high salt content, the offal could be stored for many months.

At one time, three flit boats were in use at Heogan. The originals would have been sail driven. As they had no mechanical lifting gear, a steam crane for discharging their cargos was installed on the pier. In the 1930s my father, James Tulloch, was crane driver having served as crane boy on the north boats.

During my early years at Heogan, I was fortunate to have Davie White, then an elderly man, as a workmate. From him, and Father, I got an insight into how it had been in the past. Davie had been employed as oilman at the factory in the 1930's. He explained how, during storage, oil separated naturally. Davies responsibility had been to recover the so called 'float oil' from the pits, using a steam 'dunkey' pump or a huge ladle with a long wooden handle. The recovered oil was pumped into settling tanks, where water and impurities were drained from the bottom. The oil was then filled into barrels or steel drums ready for dispatch.

Davie was still looking after the fish oil tanks in the 1950s, saying that it was the most important job, as it was from the oil that profits were made.

The original process was very labour intensive. Following the recovery of float oil, the remaining residue was cooked in what was described as 'the digester' – a batch cooker. Cooking was by steam injection. When a batch was duly cooked, it was emptied into wooden vats and then 'ladled' into strong hessian bags. The bags of cooked mass were folded over and stacked into a hydraulic press, in alternate layers of bags, woven basket mats and steel plates. Hydraulic pressure was then applied to extract the liquid. After pressing, the bags were shaken out by hand, cleaned and made ready for reuse. Handling bags of scalding mass must have been a hazardous task.

The press cake was conveyed to a flame drier and then piled up. At the end of the season it was ground and bagged as fertiliser, as the name British Oil & Guano Co. suggests. High protein fish meal, as we know it, was not produced at Heogan until 1946. Fish oil, the high value end product, was used in soap manufacture, leather tanning and other industrial uses.

The original process was still in use in the early 1930s - it can therefore be assumed that little had changed at Heogan during the first fifty years.

Here are some recollections from bygone days. The first is extracts from the unpublished autobiography of Elizabeth J. Smith (née Anderson) and is shown here with kind permission of her daughter, Stella Sutherland.

> *My father at this period had secured work at a "guano" factory which had been built in 1883 at Heogan Bressay, to utilise the herring offal from the numerous and at that time, prosperous, herring stations. The fish curers were only too glad to get this hitherto useless extra removed, so with aid of machinery-boilers, hydraulic presses, and mills – it was converted, after various grades of oil had been drawn off, into fertiliser.*
>
> *The best quality of oil was that which rose to the surface of the "midden" where the offal was dumped. The next grade was obtained after boiling and so on.*

My uncle Donnie Tulloch in the 1930s. Bressay Heritage Centre

The work was unbelievably filthy, but also, for some reason, unbelievably healthy. Several men who had suffered from rheumatism and troubles of that type, got completely rid of their aches and pains – a thing which my father attributed to sweating in the steaming air of the presses, and then being almost literary soaked in herring oil, which ran willy-nilly up their arms and dripped on their shoulders from the hydraulic presses, when they reached up to extract the caked and glutinous residue. Some of the oil went to soap factories; some to railways; and the fertiliser to various companies which dealt in these aids to agriculture.

More modern machinery has long since been installed; and the offal is no longer free for the taking. My father worked in the factory for ten years, at a weekly wage of 18/9. His clothes were dreadful to wash and lasted no time, and his boots lasted only a few weeks, owing to the nature of the stuff they worked among, which perished the leather.

He rose at 4 o'clock every morning (save Sunday) and left the house at 5 o'clock, tramping the three miles to Heogan to be ready to start in good time at 6am.

The man referred to, was Thomas Anderson (1859 -1940s) of the Old Manse, Bressay. The period referred to is approximately 1904. (EJS does not give exact dates).

Bertie Smith – looking back.

Bertie was born at Heogan in 1909. He grew up there and, as a youth, worked at the factory. After living and working in Aberdeen for some time, he returned to Bressay with his wife and family. Bertie established a car hire and haulage firm on Bressay. Later, he and Jeanie took over the Bressay shop, which they ran successfully until they retired. Here is a copy of Bertie's story which can be seen at Bressay Heritage Centre. It is reproduced here with kind permission of his daughter, Marjorie Thomson.

All the boys living in Heogan used to watch for the stock boat coming to Cruester with empty barrels for the summer season. We got one shilling for half a days work rolling the barrels up the pier. 'The boys had been working outside on the croft'.

I started working full time during the herring season, when I was seventeen. That year, 1926, my father broke his ankle, when the voar and peat cutting was coming on. Then my mother and I had to start delling lay ground in March, and we delled for over two months, every day except Sundays, doing the cabbage yards last.

I got a job at the Herring Meal Factory for the summer months. I got sixpence an hour working from 6am to 6pm, with one hour off, 8-9 o'clock, and 12 midday for meals, working five days, and on Saturday 6am to 1pm.

My first job was running up the bogies on rails from the flit boat to the factory. Every bogie held four barrels. They were taken out of the boats; two at the time with can hooks, and lifted with a small steam crane that used to run on rails to the point of the pier. When the bogie reached the factory the barrels were lifted up and taken with friction lift to a platform where they were rolled towards the pits. A man took out the head of each barrel, and herring and offal was dumped into the concrete pits until it was needed. Then when the pits were full and the season coming to an end, the offal was dug out by two men with forks into a big boiler and boiled.

The following year there were two flit boats employed during the night to take the offal and broken herring to the factory pier. The boats were ex-herring fishing boats about 50 feet long. There were two of a crew in each boat. These men slept during daytime, and I got a job with an older man an ex-whaler, to discharge the boats. We had to go into the hold and hook in the barrels with can hooks, two at a time. It was slippery standing on the greasy barrels.

Big Geordie Nelson, as we called him, was over six foot tall, and while we worked he would tell me of his experience

Trimming the pits, Geordie Tulloch right. During the 1930s.

Bressay Heritage Centre

at the Arctic whaling. When a whale was sighted, his boat was the first one to be launched and row off to where the whale was. He was a great reader and gave me a loan of his copy of Zane Grey's book, which if I remember rightly was Riders of the Purple Sage *the first book of Zane Grey that I read.*

My father used to go to Baltasound during the fishing season as skipper of a steam launch. This was used for towing the sail fishing boats to and from the fishing grounds on calm days."

Jock Johnston remembers.

Jock's father was Charlie Johnston who was factory manager at Heogan from 1922 until 1939. Jock, who now lives in Northampton, visited Bressay Heritage Centre some years ago and on his return home wrote an article entitled 'Bressay recollections'. His article can be seen at the Heritage Centre. With Jock's permission, here are some extracts from his story.

Boilerman Jock Johnston, Charlie's father.
Bressay Heritage Centre

"I was born on 9th August 1923 at the factory house Heogan, about a year after my father, Charlie Johnston, took over as factory manager. My early memories appear to be the reek from the herring drifters going out the north Mouth and watching the becalmed sailing boats trying to brace the incoming tide in the north harbour.

At the time of my birth the factory was owned by The British Oil and Guano Company, who eventually sold out in the mid 1930s to Herring By Products. At that time there was another "gut" factory at Aiths Voe. At Heogan the offal was collected from curing stations around the harbour by three factory owned boats, the Glenurie, *a former steam drifter altered, a converted Fifie the* Oceanic *and a sailing boat the* Ivy. *Many exiting episodes were performed by the* Ivy *whose skipper wasn't the worlds' best judge of speed. Collisions with piers were frequent.*

There were eight herring curing stations based in Bressay; White and Willows, Eddie Gordon, Stuart Dothie, P & W Buchan and Willie Dothie.

I can't remember who was at Cruester, but Moore's was at Leirness and Jenkins at Ham. In the early 1930s Eddie Gordon moved across the harbour and his station at Heogan was taken over by the German "Freshers". A large store of boxes was kept there and two steamers the John Raeder *and* Freda Raeder, *both from Altona, plied between Bressay and Hamburg. Their herring was laid down in boxes and heavily iced. As young lads we had a small business going with both*

Manager Charlie Johnson, with wife and child.   *Bressay Heritage Centre*

ships captains. We scoured Heogan and Beosetter, even on
occasions Gunnista for eggs – as many as we could get.

    In the summer when both boats operated we could buy
eggs for six pence a dozen and sell them for eight pence a
dozen – two pence a dozen was a handsome profit in those
days."

Jock has kindly sent me an update where he remembers how it was in
the old factory. Here are some further extracts, which are supplemented
by a sketch of the site and another of the machinery layout.

    The main engine was a large single stoke unit with
a fifteen foot diameter, five ton flywheel. The trick when
shutting down the engine was to get the stroke arm just
beyond the centre. If you mistimed the stroke, the flywheel
had to be manually turned to bring it back into position; it
took six men to do it! Just behind the main engine room was
the dynamo room. The generator, driven by a beautiful little
steam engine, developed 110 volts DC. It was used throughout
the night and quite often in daytime, for although, there
were skylights running the full length of the ridge, it could
get quite dark on a dull summers day.

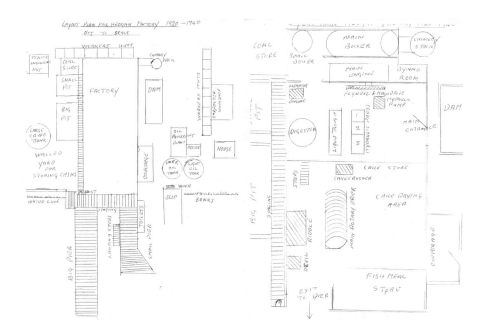

Jock Johnston's sketches. Left the site, right machines layout.

Jock describes the main drive shaft, twenty feet above ground level, and the difficulties experienced with belts coming off. He describes the process which differs only slightly from that already outlined.

With regard to fish oil he says:

There were two types of oil; light and dark .The light oil was most valuable. It was used in the manufacture of a variety of foodstuff, especially margarine. The dark oil had a lower value and was widely used in the manufacture of steel. I well remember shiploads of forty gallon casks heading for Chicago, the home of the American car industry.

Heogan factory, 1925. From left – back: Geordie Smith, Jamie Cheyne, unknown, unknown, ? Wiseman, Jamie Eunson, Robbie Eunson. 2nd row: first seven unknown, Peter Johnson (Sandwick), unknown, "Shakin" Willie Smith. 3rd Row: unknown, Tammy Anderson?, unknown, Robbie Moncrieff (Hillside, Heogan), Charlie Johnson, next six unknown, Lowrie Morrison, Fiddler: Front: Jamie Smith "Vance" (Bertie's father), boy John Johnson, unknown, Geordie Tulloch, two unknown, boy Charles Johnson, Charles Johnson, Charlie Stove, Willie Thomson, Jamie McDonald, unknown.

Bressay Heritage Centre

3

LEAN TIMES AND GLUT

WHEN the winter herring fishery on the Norwegian coast failed in the early 1930s, misfortune in Norway led to a revival at Heogan. In 1934, a fish meal and oil factory on the island of Stord got virtually no supplies. The factory owner Sigfinn Bartz-Johannessen was a man with foresight and vision. He knew that huge quantities of herring offal were being dumped into the sea in Shetland and Fraserburgh while two factories owned by British Oil & Guano Company (BOGO) lay dormant. Was it possible to get this surplus material to Norway?

Sigfinn made a proposal to the Aberdeen based company, Leslie & Co., who were involved in the salt herring trade. Leslie's reaction was positive, and on 15th May 1935 Herring By Products Ltd. (HBP) was formed. Twenty percent of the share capital was taken up by Leslie & Co., and the remaining eighty percent by S. Bartz-Johannessen. At the outset, the board members were Sigfinn Bartz-Johannessen, Charles McLachlan, John E. Todd and Hugo Arnesen.

Both factories were out of use in 1935, but it is unclear when BOGO stopped trading. HBP bought the two factories from BOGO and a new chapter in the Heogan story began.

Replacement of the primitive machinery at both factories was desirable but unviable. A decision was reached to supplement the existing machinery with used plant from Norwegian factories on Stord and Sotra.

The Heogan and Fraserburgh factories were prepared for production once more. During 1936-37, a flame drier was installed at Heogan and two steam driers at Fraserburgh. With the primitive production method still in use, neither factory had the capacity to process a large volume of offal.

In 1937 Norwegian boats were chartered for the transportation of offal to Norway. A disused concrete coal hulk, anchored in Lerwick north harbour, was used for storage of offal prior to export. The hulk was unstable when loaded with an almost liquid cargo of offal and would suddenly take a list.

Offal was also stored in the pits at Heogan, awaiting shipment to Norway. A reversible fish conveying system was set up on the north side of the pier to facilitate the intake and dispatches at Heogan. During the next few years, a considerable amount of offal was shipped to Norway.

With the outbreak of World War II on 3rd September 1939, the Scottish and Shetland fishing industries were severely curtailed. When the German invasion of Norway followed on 9th April 1940, all links with the mother company in Bergen were severed and HBP was forced to stop trading.

The Heogan factory was requisitioned by the War Commission, as was a disused herring curer's yard and wooden pier at Cruester, about half a mile south of Heogan. There, eight cylindrical fuel tanks, each with capacity of 12,000 gallons, were concealed below ground level, encased

in sand, bricks and concrete. The tanks were used to store fuel for the Motor Torpedo Boats based in Lerwick.

George Brooks, a Londoner now residing in Bressay, was a young man in the Royal Navy. Stationed at Heogan, his job was to refuel the M.T.B. boats at the old pier at Cruester. During the war years, the workers' huts at Heogan were used as accommodation for the men who tended the fuel tanks.

At the end of the war little could be done at Heogan while the War Office held control of the property. In 1945 Christian Bartz-Johannessen attended meetings with the Ministry of Food, in London and also on Shetland. Eventually the property was released. Christian became a director of the company in 1946.

George Brooks, Bressay, about 1943.
George Brooks

In April that year, a consignment of used machinery from Norway arrived at Heogan onboard the fishing vessel *Gullhorn*. The cargo included a flame drier which had been used to make coffee substitute during the war. Skilled workers were sent from Norway to install the machinery and supervise the production

The Fraserburgh Factory lay dormant during the war years. It was suspected that the 100 feet high chimney at the factory was used as a navigational aid by German bombers. On 4th June 1941 the factory was bombed, causing much damage but the chimney remained intact. The factory, however, was classified a total loss. At the end of the war, a claim was made to the War Damage Commission. Their decition was that compensation payable to HBP would be £2.200 net.

In 1946, Joe Campbell, who had been foreman before the war, was appointed manager at Fraserburgh. His first duty was to repair the factory and get the machinery operational, following the destruction caused by the German bomber.

With revival of the herring fishery in 1946, the Ministry of Food guarantied fishermen a minimum price of £12 per cran of herring delivered to the factories. But the offer was unattractive. Later that year the industry got a great boost when The Herring Industry Board (HIB) was set up by the Government. Its role was to encourage revival of the fishery.

HIB organised a scheme known as 'The Pool'. Fishermen were paid a flat rate for herring, irrespective of its end use. A bonus was payable at the end of the season depending the Board's profit. The scheme worked well for all concerned. After the various outlets for human consumption had been met, the balance went for meal and oil. A contract was set up with HBP to process the surplus fish at a fixed price per cran and HIB agreed to pay all the factory expenses during the season.

With the intervention of HIB, herring arriving in abundance. Forty six drifters fished in Shetland waters during the 1946 season, their catch amounting to 63,000 crans of which 5,964 crans (about 1,000 tons) went for meal & oil. Heogan got a great boost through the new agreement, which encouraged local fishermen to deliver to the factory.

As herring quality was unsuitable for curing until June, the fleet fished exclusively for the factory during the whole month of May.

The contract with HIB worked well, and continued until 1960. The factory operated during the herring season from May till September. At the end of the season all the workers were paid off, but many came back year after year.

4

THE 1950S – PART ONE

A SMARTLY dressed, relatively young man rushed passed, out the door and was gone. Later, I discovered that the man in a hurry was manager George Wills, or to be correct, ex-manager. He had just finished, as I started my first 12 hour nightshift at Heogan at 6pm on 18th May 1955.

It was the first time I had stepped through the factory door but, like everyone else on the island, I was well accustomed to the smell when the wind was blowing from the north.

No-one came to give me instructions and I was unsure of what to do. A notice board with a list of employees and their job titles caught my eye. The last name on the list was J. H. Tulloch, 'fireman'.

Making my way to the boiler room I found Magnie Yates shovelling coal into the steam boiler. He seemed to be making heavy work of it, with sweat pouring down his face. Magnie assumed that I had been assigned as his assistant and set me to work to wheel in coal for him. By the time that the shift foreman, George Wilmot, came looking for me Magnie had a pile of coal delivered.

"What are you doing here?" asked George.

"I saw my name listed as fireman."

"It is not this fire that you have to look after; it's the one in the cookhouse. You have to make tea for the boys and by the way, there's a

Magnie Yates, Bressay, 1955.   *Eva Yates*

radio in there. Listen to the local fleet and make a list of the likely herring landings here tomorrow." At least there was something more to do than just making tea for the boys.

As expected, a letter from the Ministry of Defence arrived with instructions to report to the T.A. Hall in Lerwick for a National Service medical. The examining doctor asked: "Why are you limping?"

Surprised that he had noticed the limp, my brief explanation was: "My leg is sore."

The doctor wrote something on a form, and then looked at me thoughtfully for a moment before concluding: "I am sending you to Greyfriar's House, Aberdeen, for further examination".

The verdict of the three man team of doctors in Aberdeen was, 'Unfit for military service'.

I made an appointment with my doctor in Lerwick and asked: "Can you tell me why I have pains in this leg? I also get severe stomach cramp, which has been going on for some time."

"Oh, it's just the result of the polio," said Dr. Mackenzie.

"Polio, when did I have polio?"

"Did they not tell you when you were so ill in Orkney?" he asked, adding that it was probably for the best that I had not been told, as getting moving again was the best and only treatment.

I became more concerned: "Will it get worse?"

"No. Some muscles are paralysed, but you will find that other muscles will take over, and you will get used to it. As a consolation, you will never contract polio again."

The leg gradually became stronger and the stomach cramps eventually subsided. Polio had left me with a handicap however; apart from a limp I could no longer push a barrow uphill. Fortunately, Magnie's coal barrow had been on the flat.

As military service was now ruled out, I asked for a proper job in the factory. Three weeks of making tea on night shift was quite enough.

Sandy Cardno, a full time employee at the Fraserburgh factory, had been working for some weeks at Heogan as a stand-in separator operator. Sandy wanted to return home and so, after one week's training, I had a proper job and Sandy happily went back to Fraserburgh.

The separator station became my workplace for the summer seasons of 1955 to 1957. It was not as Robbie Sinclair had described his vocation, 'money for old rope'. My job was more work intensive, but it was one of the best-paid jobs in the factory.

Here is a copy of a pay sheet from 30th May 1956 showing details of employees' earnings, and from memory, their job descriptions.

Name	Job	From	Rate of pay	Hours worked	Gross pay £ S D
C. Taylor,	Manager	Fraserburgh	£ 11/ Wk		11 00 00
A. G. White	Assistant Manager	Bressay	4/- hr	88 ½	23 17 00
J. Campbell	Foreman	Fraserburgh	4/- hr	78	20 12 00
I. Summers	Foreman	Bressay	4/- hr	91	
D. White	Oil man	Bressay	3/9 ,,	77	18 13 01
J. McDonald	Tally man	Bressay	3/9 ,,	48	9 07 06
R. Anderson	Handy man	Sullom	3/9 ,,	62 ½	13 00 10
C. H. McDonald	Skipper	Bressay	3/9 ,,	73 ½	17 10 07
W. Morgan	Boiler man	Uncertain	3/9 ,,	89 ½	22 15 05
M. Yates	Boiler man	Bressay	3/9 ,,	73	17 18 06
John Johnston	Separators	Dunrossness	3/9 ,,	75	18 07 10
J. H. Tulloch	Separators	Bressay	3/9 ,,	89 ½	22 15 05
J. Wiseman	Flit boat	Lerwick	3/8 ,,	73 ½	17 02 10
W. Watt	Flit boat	Lerwick	3/8 ,,	73 ½	17 02 10
R. Hansen	Launch driver	Mossbank	3/7 ,,	97	23 08 06
J. Jamieson	Day worker	Uncertain	3/7 ,,	77	18 00 01
Jas. Johnston	Day worker	Uncertain	3/7 ,,	72	16 09 08
J. R. Smith	Odd job man	Bressay	3/7 ,,	44	06 12 00
G. Tulloch	Press man	Bressay	3/7 ,,	89 ½	21 15 09
A. W. Priest	Loft man	Yell	3/7 ,,	88 ½	21 10 04
J. Linklater	Meal store	Bressay	3/7 ,,	89	22 04 08
J. C. Henry	Pits	Bressay	3/7 ,,	89	22 04 08
E. Reid	Pits	Culswick	3/7 ,,	86 ½	20 13 00
G. Smith	Drier man	Levenwick	3/7 ,,	90	21 19 04
A. Duncan	Spare man	Uncertain	3/7 ,,	88 ½	21 15 09
P. Sandilands	Loft man	Bressay	3/7 ,,	67 ½	15 00 02
John. Bairnson	Pits	Dunrossness	3/7 ,,	83 ½	20 08 10
R. Sinclair	Drier man	Bressay	3/7 ,,	75	17 11 09
J. R. Williamson	Cooker	Yell	3/7 ,,	75	17 11 09
G. Eunson	Spare man	Dunrossness	3/7 ,,	78	18 07 11
J. Manson	Meal store	Bressay	3/7 ,,	78	18 07 11
R. Robertson	Meal store	Brunthammersland	3/7 ,,	76 ½	17 19 10
W. Manson	Pits	Bressay	3/7 ,,	78	18 07 11
W. Laurenson	Pits	Bressay	3/7 ,,	78	18 07 11
W. Leask	Pits	Bressay	3/7 ,,	72	16 15 00
A. Hoseason	Spare man	Yell	3/7 ,,	76 ½	17 19 10
Mrs M. White	Cook	Bressay		-	8 00 00
Mrs Wilson	Assistant Cook	Lerwick		-	6 00 00
				TOTAL PAID OUT FOR THE WEEK	£ 668 10 06

Checking the oil tanks was Davy White's responsibility, but I was soon doing the legwork while Davy looked after the separators. It was a welcome opportunity to get out for fresh air. Fish oil solidifies when cold, and I spent several nights stoking the small coal fired boiler at the original tank site at Cruester, prior to shipping out the oil by sea tanker. The tanks were relocated on a site adjacent to the Freshers pier in 1957.

Davy was a fine old man. He had many amusing events to recall. Speaking one day on that inexhaustible topic, Shetlands weather, Davy referred to an elderly Bressay woman, who said:

"It usually comes some kind o' wader about dis time o' year."

There was a period in the late 1950s when little herring was being caught by the Shetland driftnet fleet. Davy's comment was:

"You need not look for herring with this northerly wind. I have seen it all before."

Sure enough, when the wind changed to southerly there was plenty of herring to be found.

Davy would frequently weigh himself on the scales, which were used to weigh oil drums. One day, as he stepped off the scales, I enquired:

"What weight are you today Davy?"

"Oh just about da twa hunder–weight. Hit never varies very much, maybe a pound or twa up or doon."

The machinery in use at Heogan in 1955 was old and ineffective; it was simply cast-offs from Norwegian factories, or from the Fraserburgh factory. To make a first class product from old and often decaying fish was almost impossible.

MV *Valorous* was the flit boat in use at the time. She was owned by the factory and had a three-man crew; Hector Macdonald, 'Heckie', son

Two of my workmates in the 1950s. Johnnie Dalziel, Bressay (left), and Peter Manson, Bressay.   *Andy Dalziel and Peter Manson Jr.*

of former factory manager James Macdonald, was her skipper. Herring offal was collected daily from a string of curing stations extending along Lerwick waterfront. The barrels were emptied into the boat's open hold by the crew.

On arrival at the factory, an additional five men were required to discharge the cargo. Four men went into the hold using forks and shovels to fill the offal into Norwegian-manufactured wooden tubs, each with 100 litre capacity. The skipper operated the lifting mechanism which was simply a rope with several turns on the drum end of the boat's winch. His two crew members operated the guy ropes. While the second tub was being filled in the hold, man number eight tipped the tub into the conveyor.

The conveyers and pits were uncovered. As a result, many tons of fish went to feed the seagulls that congregated in their thousands. The storage pits were divided into three compartments, with a combined capacity of approximately 350 tonnes. A team of three manned the pits on each shift. Their job was to feed a conveyer using forks, shovels and wheel barrows. It was hard and dirty work. The pit men on my shift were all called 'Willie': Laurenson, Leask, and Manson. They were all characters and were constantly poking fun at each other.

A timber-cased scraper conveyor elevated the fish from the pits to a hopper on the loft. From there it travelled through an open screw conveyor to the cooker. Fish intake was regulated by the loft man, who controlled the intake by ringing a ship's bell. The signal was two bells to start feeding the conveyer and one bell to stop. He could also stop the conveyer by an emergency stop button, as could the pit men. In addition to controlling the fish intake, the loft man dosed the fish with formaldehyde which aided the binding process.

The cooker, on a lower level, was simply an encased screw conveyer, about 8 metres long x 70 cm diameter. Live steam was injected into the cooker, with the result that poor quality fish was reduced to soup, making the next stage of the process almost impossible. The dewatering device was an inclining screw conveyor in an encased perforated screen, but it was ineffective and acted like an agitator. The resulting 'fish soup' poured onto the floor, sometimes for hours on end.

I remember one 12 hour shift when not a single bag of meal was produced. The entire product simply poured onto the floor, down a flight of concrete steps and out the lower door, eventually flowing into the sea. In extreme circumstances it was necessary to wear three quarter length rubber boots to walk through the mess.

The Pits – full to the brim during the 1950s.   *Bartz-Johannessen*

Geordie Tulloch looked after the single screw press. Like the cooker it was old and ineffective, adding to the poor overall end result. Geordie and several others walked three miles to work and, after being on their feet for a twelve hour shift, walked home again. My granduncle, Willie Birnie, worked in the meal store during the 1950s. Willie could be seen starting his long walk home carrying a huge hank of herring. He was a kind and considerate man and gave a few herring to anyone he met. By the time he arrived home there were no herring left.

The product was split after going through the press. The solids were conveyed by screw conveyers to a flame drier, passing through a very noisy pulverizer èn route. The liquid, following separation of solids, was pumped to a tank above the separators. After working a 12 hr shift next to that noisy pulverizer, I could hear the sound in my head many hours later. Little wonder that my hearing is not good today. It was necessary to dismantle and clean the two manual operated separators frequently, and the oil purifier was done weekly.

The drier consisted of a brick furnace fired by two diesel injection burners, using steam as an atomiser. Hot air from the furnace entered the drying chamber, assisted by a suction fan at the outlet end. The drying chamber was a revolving horizontal steel drum, suspended on four rollers. It was driven by an electric motor via a gear box and cogwheels. The drier drum was about 10 metres long x 1.4 metres diameter. Paddles inside the drum gave the impression of a cement mixer.

The damp gases were extracted by the suction fan, passing through a cyclone to extract dust before being discharged to the atmosphere. It was not uncommon for the drier to go on fire, and water was laid on to extinguish the flames.

The dry matter was conveyed overhead pneumatically via another cyclone, prior to grinding and bagging in the meal store. Two men were employed in the meal store. They filled and sewed the bags, weighing them first to ensure that there was exactly one hundredweight in each. Prior to stowing, the bags were set out in rows to cool for 12 hours.

As the meal price was based on 70% protein, the aim was to achieve the maximum allowable moisture content of 10%. If the moisture exceeded 10%, or if the meal had not been properly cooled, it would generate heat and at the worst, take fire.

The meal store men on my shift were Dovie Linklater from Beosetter, and Robbie Robertson from Brunthamersland, commonly known as 'Robbie o' Wham'. They were both characters, and full of fun. They knew the moisture content of the meal by its bulk. If the moisture was too high it was impossible to get one hundredweight in the bag. Occasionally when I stood in as drier operator, Robbie would wander slowly across from the meal store with the message: "Dovie says it's a bit damp."

One day when things got completely out of hand, Robbie came running across at full speed and, without making reference to Dovie, described the moisture content in unprintable terms. Robbie had many stories to tell. He was always quiet on Mondays, but as the days passed, his stories became more and more prolific with the thought of the approaching weekend.

Robbie Robertson, Brunthamarsland.
Neil Anderson

Dovie became a permanent worker in 1957; He was an optimist, never complaining about anything. His turn of phrase and his hilarious antics often lightened the mood and made the factory a happier workplace. He retired for health reasons in January 1964.

The fireman's job was undoubtedly the most important one in the factory as the entire process depended on his ability to maintain a constant steam pressure of 80psi. Magnie Yates often struggled to keep the pressure up, whereas Bill Morgan, on the opposite shift, was an expert, making the work look effortless.

One day George Wilmot, the foreman, suspecting that the pressure had dropped, went to investigate. A quick look at the pressure gauge was enough; it registered 20psi. George exploded.

"Magnie, just look at that, what to hell is going on here?"

"Oh yons da second time roond." was Magnie's quick and witty reply.

I had known Magnie all my life and was very fond of him; he had lost an eye as a boy when he fell on a broken bottle. Magnie was slow in his movements but never slow with an answer. He had a great sense of humour and sometimes set the scene for fun at his own expense.

One morning, while we were at breakfast in the canteen, Magnie dropped his fork on the floor and lamented: "Oh dear, will I have to bend?"

Willie Manson, who could be quite sarcastic, cut in like lightning: "Na Magnie, don't do bend whatever do does, do might brak."

Magnie just grinned; he would soon get his own back.

Some years earlier, Willie had applied for an advertised job as ploughman at Hoversta farm on Bressay. He was, however, unaccustomed to handling the huge Clydesdale horses and had great difficulty in getting their harness on. His first attempt at ploughing left a lot to be desired and the farmer had to ask his son to straighten up the furrow before folk came to the Kirk on Sunday.

We were seated at the canteen table once more, when Magnie started:

"When I's wis ploughing in Yorkshire."

(He always referred to himself as I's). Magnie had worked on a farm in Yorkshire for a time, but whether he ever did any ploughing is debatable.

Willie Manson, Bressay 1950s.
Laurence Anderson

Willie took the bait: "When to hell did do ever plough in Yorkshire?"

Magnie laid down his fork and knife and, looking Willie straight in the eye, retorted: "Weel, at least, I's don't believe dat a horse is lik a minister, and pit on his collar arse first."

Willies got a red face and the rest of the meal was eaten in silence.

One day when the pits were empty, the pit men were instructed to clean out the settling sump. This was a most undesirable job. The sump was a relic of the past, never serving any useful purpose that I could see. While they were removing the lid, a scorie descended into the 'cesspool'. Willie Laurenson, nicknamed Dutchie, with all good intentions went to rescue the bird, but unfortunately he slipped and fell in also. Willie Leask thought it hilarious; he could hardly speak as he revealed the tale of woe. The unfortunate fellow was close behind, requesting my help to get cleaned up. He was hosed down first, and then stripped.

In all my life I have never seen anyone so dirty or smelling like Willie Laurenson did that day. I remember that it was on a Friday, as Willie's pay packet was still in his pocket. The money had to be washed too, as the pay packet was soaked through. His clothes were washed in the usual manner of boiling them in a solution of washing soda with the aid of a steam pipe. But I suspect that was their last wash.

Many amusing events were created by Dutchie, whose standard expression was 'Holy Sailor' if something was surprising to him (which was most of the time). One afternoon the cook had been baking. At the sight of home bakes, Dutchie's face lit up,

Rasmie Reid, Culswick, at 88 years of age.   *Robert Johnson*

Roald Hanson, Mossbank. Arne Hansen

"Holy sailor. Fancies! How many apiece?"

The workers from Lerwick and the surrounding area were able to go home after work; those from further afield were the bothy boys. The bothy was a rectangular, corrugated iron clad building sub divided into three units, each with accommodation for four men. It was warm and cosy in the bothy, thanks to the cast iron coal fired bogies with a hob on top for the tea kettle.

If possible, the boys went home for Saturday night and returned on Sunday, either to start nightshift on Sunday or at 6am on Monday morning.

An old hand, who came back year after year, was Rasmie Reid from Culswick. Jackie Johnston (Togsie), Tammie Aitken, Jamie and John Bairnson and Robbie Leask were all from Dunrossness. Geordie Leslie came from Levenwick. Others from Mossbank were James John Cooper, Bertie Cooper and Tammie Peterson and Roald Hansen.

Roald, a Norwegian, had fled Norway in 1940 in a British destroyer when the battle of Narvik ended. Seventeen years old at the time he was trained in Air-sea rescue and posted to Sullom Voe in 1943 to join the Norwegian Naval Air force 330 squadron. After the war, he returned to Shetland where he married Ruby Irvine and settled in Mossbank.

Roald, (who stayed in Lerwick during the week), was for a time my opposite number as separator man. Later he became driver of the factory launch.

Andrew Mullay, Bigton.   Drew Mullay

The Yell boys were John R. Williamson, Ewan and Willie Moar, and from Brunthamersland, Robbie Robertson. Then there was Andrew Mullay from Bigton; he was a great cartoonist and fiddle player. I had bought a tape recorder (the first in Bressay), which became a great source of entertainment in addition to Andrew's fiddle. I found new friends in the Bothy boys, spending many enjoyable evenings in their company. Coming as they did from different areas in Shetland, it was enlightening to listen to their stories and hear of their experiences.

Some of my new-found friends were regular visitors at East Ham, where they were always made welcome by my parents. It was a change for the boys to get away from the factory for a few hours. Togsie and the Mossbank boys were regular visitors. If some croft work had to be done they were always willing to help, having a lot of fun in the process.

My first mode of transport was a bicycle, which was soon replaced by an auto bike. Lacking power, the 98cc engine required assistance from the pedals when climbing hills.

An old Norton motorbike proved to be a poor investment, constantly breaking down. Eventually it went on fire, so no more repairs were required. The next upgrade was a 250cc B.S.A., which was in good condition. It had a windscreen and leg shields for added comfort in all sorts of weather

Few of my workmates at that time owned even a bicycle. They simply walked the three miles to work for a 6am start, and after doing a 12 hour shift, walked home again. It is not surprising that an offer of a lift was greatly appreciated. I had various passengers on a regular basis including Willie Manson, his brother Jamie, Geordie Yates and Magnie Fraser.

One morning I had overslept and was in a hurry to get to work on time. Magnie Fraser was my passenger that morning. I was driving faster than normal and could feel my passenger getting tense. When I laid the bike over to take a certain corner Magnie lost his nerve and leaned in the opposite direction. Struggling to stay on the road, I had to apply

Magnie Fraser, Bressay.

my weight against his. The footrest struck the road and we took a bit of a lurch. Magnie exclaimed: "Eyee there's not all that hurry".

Luckily we did not crash, but ever after when we approached that corner, my passenger just froze and I had to reduce speed to a crawl.

Geordie Yates was not an ideal pillion passenger either, he would say: "Wait till I get a good had o' de." He then steered me round every corner.

My favourite passenger was undoubtedly my mother; she was so completely relaxed. Father, on the other hand, accused me of speeding at 30 miles an hour.

In August 1955, my cousin Geordie Anderson and Pearl Deyell got married in the Bressay church, followed by a reception in the hall. It was a great wedding. The only downside was that we were working 12 hour shifts at the time. Luckily I was on day shift; it would have been unthinkable to miss the wedding. My opposite number agreed to take over from me at 3pm so that I could get cleaned up in time for the wedding at 5 o'clock.

The reception went on all night and I got home just in time to change clothes and get to work on my motorbike. Almost sleeping on my feet, I was so tired that I didn't dare sit down.

Charlie Taylor, the manager, came by to enquire: "Have you seen Magnie this morning?"

"Yes, but that was in the Bressay hall,"

"Will you take your motorbike and go see if you can find him. I will look after this lot till you get back."

It was great to get out of the factory and into the fresh air. I found Magnie at home, happily sleeping it off. After coaxing him back to life, we headed for Heogan once more. Again I arranged for my opposite number to stand in for me at 3pm, as a second night of dancing and festivities was not to be missed. After a short sleep, I returned to the hall for the second night, followed by another 12 hour shift at Heogan.

5

THE 1950S – PART TWO

WHEN I started work at Heogan, three wooden piers were being used by the factory. The so called factory pier was used for the intake of fish and also for dispatching fish meal. Herring was discharged from the boats in baskets and tipped into the conveyer. A wood cased conveyer, mounted on its north side, conveyed fish to the pits.

The second was the Fresher's Pier, some 100 metres south of the factory, where small coasters delivered coal for the steam boiler.

The third pier had (only just) survived since the days of herring curing. Situated about half a mile south of the factory, the pier and tanks had been taken over by the factory after the war. The tanks had been cleaned and were used to store fish oil. A small tanker called at the pier to collect the oil.

The factory pier was in daily use. When a chartered cargo vessel came to collect fish meal, she berthed at the south side of the factory pier. Due to the shallow water, it was necessary to berth at high tide. The ship then sat firmly, but safely on the soft seabed awaiting the next high tide.

One day, Hay and Company's *Shetland Trader* came alongside to collect fish meal. I was on the pier to take the ropes and saw the ship approaching much too fast. I had a moment of indecision, should I run for my life? However, I just stood there hoping for the best. The pier bent like a bamboo wand, only to spring back again to its original shape. Unbelievably, it was undamaged; its strength was in its flexibility.

The meal store was an ex-military, timber framed building clad in corrugated cement asbestos sheeting. About 200 tons of fishmeal could be stowed there, and a further 80 tons in a lean-to extension at the seaward end of the factory. Eighteen dockers were employed to load the ship. The younger dockers manned the two wheeled barrows, with one man in the shafts and another pushing. As they ran at full speed, it was referred to as 'The Bressay Derby'. The older members laid out rope slings, loading eight bags on each barrow. The slings were lifted onboard by ship's crane, where the remaining dockers stowed the cargo.

The dockers carried thermos flasks and sandwiches for their breaks. One day I noticed that one of them had no food with him. He looked hungry and I felt sorry for him. A boat had just delivered fresh herring and I had a few ready to take home.

"Would you like me to grill you a herring?" I asked.

His eyes lit up as he replied: "That would be great."

I found a piece of cable tray, placed it on the metal flue duct of the coal fired boiler, which resulted in an excellent grill. The hungry fellow later expressed his gratitude: "That's the best herring I have ever tasted."

From then on 'the grill' was in regular use, whenever fresh herring was available.

The smell from Heogan could be quite repulsive in Lerwick, or likewise on Bressay depending on the wind direction, but people accepted it as part of the fishing industry. SEPA did not exist and, provided that no major oil spill was seen on the harbour, few serious complaints were raised. It would be 1968 before steps were taken to reduce the smell and control the effluent discharge from the factory.

Only in 1973, when the new canteen was built, were showers provided for the workers. I was, however, more fortunate than most as father had built a washhouse just after the war. With my help, as a schoolboy, we had dug out a well on higher ground and piped water to the porch and the new washhouse where a bathtub was installed. It had all been accomplished at a minimum cost, using second hand material throughout. The peat fired range in the 'but end' supplied hot water from an internal boiler. An open fire in the wash house added to the comfort. So here I was, in the 1950s, living in luxury.

When working nightshift it often became too warm and difficult to sleep in my upstairs bedroom. I therefore moved my bed to the washhouse. Thereafter, it was simply to have a bath, jump right into bed and sleep like a log.

It seemed that the smell of Heogan got right into the pores of your skin. One night after my usual bath, having added some dettol for good measure, I put on clean clothes and went to a dance. I was dancing with an attractive stranger, when she suddenly asked: "Do you work at the Heogan factory?"

"Yes, but why do you ask?"

"I can smell it," was her answer.

In May 1957, I was back at my old job as separator operator. At the end of that season the factory became operational 12 months of the year for the first time. The workers that winter were: Andrew White, manager; Jamie Henry, foreman; Davy White; Jamie McDonald; Hector McDonald; Dovie Linklater; Willie Manson and me.

MacFisheries had started a white fish filleting factory at Brown's Road, Lerwick. Their offal was collected on a daily basis, as was offal from other smaller merchants in Lerwick and Scalloway. Iceatlantic in Scalloway was soon going full swing, producing a lot of offal. We lost out when they installed their own fish meal plant. Much later, several filleting factories were established throughout the islands.

By 1957, the old wooden pier at the tank site was falling apart. William Fraser Contractors was employed to relocate the eight tanks on a vacant spot adjacent to the Fresher's pier. The tanks were launched into the sea and towed to the new site, where they were winched and jacked into place

As the tanks were now exposed to the elements, they became prone to rust. Thereafter, 'chipping tanks' became a byword. I hated the job, which was never ending. An application of cheap bitumen paint was ineffective, and rust was showing through in no time.

I was working on top of a tank one day, with Willie Manson working below me. A wet and smelly fish meal bag had been left on the tank from the previous day. I picked up the bag and threw it, with no thought of where it would land. A gust of wind caught the smelly bag, and by sheer chance, it ended its flight wrapped firmly around Willie's head. He was hopping mad, thinking that I had done it deliberately: "Tulloch," he shouted, "Come down here at wance, do God dammed rat." I decided that it was safer to stay aloft until he calmed down. In spite of minor tiffs, we remained good friends.

In 1957, transport of offal was contracted out to J & M Shearer Ltd. Their flitboat was MV *Jeannie*. She was a 58ft keel ex-fishing boat, built in Banff in 1896. The contract with Shearer's continued until 1964, when HBP bought *Jeannie* from Magnus Shearer, and from then on operated from Heogan with a local crew.

Barrels of offal were delivered to the boat by truck and tipped into *Jeannie's* open hold. The traditional method of discharging the *Jeannie* was as it had been on the *Valorous*. Four men were required in the hold using forks or shovels to fill the Norwegian hectolitre tubs, while a fifth man tipped the tubs into the conveyor on the pier.

Alex Wiseman, Lerwick, mid-60s.

Jeannie had several different skippers during her service with Shearers. They were namely: Jock Toonie, Alex Wiseman and Willie Sales; all characters in their own right. But Willie Sales was a favourite for teasing by us young fellows. It was so easy to get him going. We would refuse to something that he had in mind and Willie would lose his temper: "I'm going to see Magnie about this, where is the phone?" He would jump on the pier and head for the office, but soon calmed down and was back again.

Regulations stated that in her role as a freight carrier, the *Jeannie* was duty bound to carry a load line certificate. Magnie Shearer therefore went through the motions of officialdom. When a Board of Trade inspector duly arrived, he took a look round the boat and asked Willie to switch on the mast headlight. Willie clicked the appropriate switch, but nothing happened. The inspector looked up at the mast, shook his head and said: "Your mast headlight is not working."

"Ah, just hang on a minute," said Willie. "It takes a start for the electricity to get to the top of the mast."

There were some hilarious episodes with Alex Wiseman too. Magnus told the tale of Alex's time sheet. When Magnus checked it one week, he found that Alex had entered more double time than was possible for the entire weekend. Magnus confronted him: "I see you have an awful lot of double time this week Alex."

Quick off the mark Alex replied: "A helliry o' fish dis week Magnie, a helliry o' fish."

Then there was the day that Alex checked the batteries in the engine room, to discover that the cells were dry. As there was no distilled water onboard, he quickly topped them up with sea water.

As with the skippers, the *Jeannie's* crew members varied. Among them were: Stewart Sales, Gordon Williamson, Albert Wiseman and Jamie Watt. While in hospital in 2008, I was pleasantly surprised to meet Jamie Watt. I had not seen him in over 40 years, and we had so much to talk about from the past. To stop us shouting across the ward, the nurses moved Jamie within earshot; thereafter communications improved. Jamie had many interesting stories to tell.

As a young man he went to the drift-net herring fishing. During the early days of the war, when the local fleet was fishing off Sumburgh, the R.A.F. (stationed at Sumburgh) provided a Spitfire for their protection against attack by enemy aircraft. When one Spitfire went back to base, it was quickly replaced by another. One day, while their guardian angel in the sky was absent, a German plane appeared but did not attack. It may have been a reconnaissance plane. Minutes later a Spitfire was on the scene again, circling the boat, as the pilot made enquiring gestures by tipping the wings. The crew guessed what was being asked, and congregated at the bow, pointing in the direction where the plane had disappeared. The Spitfire took off in the given direction at full speed. Soon, it was back and performed a victory roll. That German plane would take no more photographs.

I had known Magnus Shearer since my early days at Heogan. As time passed we became very good friends. Magnus grew up working within the fishing industry and was involved with fishing and boats throughout his working life. He took over the family herring curing business J & M Shearer Ltd., after his father. His work within the salt herring trade led to a close relationship with Associated Herring Merchants – and in turn with HBP.

When herring curing came to an end J & M Shearer Ltd was forced to diversify – and in 1970 HBP became financially involved. Shearers owned the ice factory in Lerwick which consisted of a block ice clant and cold store and also a flake ice plant. A further flake ice plant was added in 1972 which enabled ice to be delivered directly into the fishing boats. The ice plants were great assets to the fishing fleet.

By then Shearers had diversified as shipping agents, shipbrokers and steve-dores. The local engineering company – T. W. Laurenson – was bought and incorporated into J & M Shearer Ltd. in 1975. The engineering supply company – George Boyd – became involved, and as a joint venture traded as Boyd & Shearer (Shetland) Ltd.

By 1984 HBP became overstretched by combined capital investment ventures, and a number of their subsidiary companies were sold off.

Lerwick Harbour Trust bought all of the Garthspool property. John Smith, the manager of the Shipping Division bought the assets and set up a new company known as Shearers Shipping Ltd.

Magnus Shearer.
Magnus Shearer Jr.

Magnus Shearer junior bought back the ice factory assets, trading as J & M Shearer (Ice supplies) Ltd. After one year's trading, Magnus sold out to LHD and joined that company as a director.

Sandy Laurenson and Sonny Mullay bought back the assets of T. W. Laurenson and continued to trade as L&M Engineering.

At Heogan, we had a long standing working relationship with Tommy Laurenson and his son Sandy. They were very reliable and gave an excellent service. The night of a Bressay wedding comes to mind when I was unable to attend. Tommy, Sandy and I worked throughout the night repairing a breakdown on the fish intake conveyer. The results of our efforts gained one more nights fishing for the fleet, before the season came to an end.

Shearer Shipping Ltd. was sold to SBS at Norscot Base when John Smith retired. The ice factory and ice plants in Lerwick and Scalloway were incorporated into the LHD subsidiary company LHD Marine Supplies Ltd. and L&M continues to trade as marine engineers.

James Christie Henry and I both started work at Heogan on 18th May 1955. Jamie was born at Cullivoe, Yell, in 1920 and went to sea at the age of 16. He sailed on an ammunition carrier during the early years of the war. When his father was dying Jamie was home on compassionate leave. After the funeral he reported to Lerwick labour exchange where he was told that his ship had been sunk. He'd had a lucky escape. As there were no jobs for seamen available, he was sent to Sullom Voe to work for contractor Magnie Pearson.

After the war he went to the Antarctic whaling. He later worked as an insurance agent in Edinburgh for a time. When home on holiday he met his former employer in Lerwick and accepted an offer to work as foreman on a housing scheme in Yell.

His first job at Heogan was in the pits, then as a plant operator and eventually shift foreman. I worked as a plant operator on his shift for some time and we got on well together. Jamie rented a croft in Bressay where he settled with his wife and family. I spent many enjoyable evenings with them in their new home at Beosetter.

Jamie had picked up a smattering of Norwegian at the Antarctic whaling and I learned my first Norwegian words from him.

We had a lot of fun at Heogan in those days. In spite of the adverse smell and at times getting very dirty, it was a good workplace. The company's name, Herring By Products Ltd was displayed in bold letters on the seaward end of the factory. One day, Jamie and I were walking up the pier after discharging the *Jeannie* and as usual had got very dirty. Jamie looked up at the company sign, shook his head, and said, "Herring By-Products elted!"

Jamie Henry in 1968.

"Herring By-Products elted!".

Hector Macdonald (Heckie) had worked at Heogan for many years. He was born and bred at Heogan, son of manager James Macdonald. Heckie didn't like wearing oilskins. We were working outside one day when it started to rain. I had seen by the look of the sky that a heavy shower was brewing, and had fetched my oilskins. Heckie, however, didn't turn a hair, and just carried on working. After some time the shower turned into a downpour. Eventually he looked up at the sky and muttered: "Oh well, I suppose I better go get the oilskins."

"You needn't bother now, Heckie," I said, "you're already soaked to the skin."

Maybe the reason why it took so long for the rain to penetrate his clothes was that they were so dirty, and partially waterproof. His trousers, when dry, could almost stand up by themselves. He didn't mind getting dirty; in fact I think he enjoyed it.

When Heckie thought it was time to change his trousers, he would come to me at the oil separators with the discarded ones, asking politely if I would wash them. The normal way to wash his trousers was to boil them in a washing soda solution. One day, when they were really dirty, I used caustic soda, which may well have been their last wash.

Joe Smith was another Heogan boy who worked at the factory for some years in the late 1950s and early 1960s. His family home was at Brae, Heogan. Provided that he had not had too many drams, Joe was a very good fiddle player. He was an ex-whaler, and when he got a peerie dram would often break into sentimental Norwegian songs at the top of his voice.

On days when there was no fish to process, we normally had an hour's break at one o'clock. Sometimes, to break the monotony in the canteen, Joe was persuaded to bring his fiddle. One beautiful summer's days comes to mind, when Joe was not really interested in playing his fiddle; he wanted to go over the hill to look to his peats. Just to wind him up, we said that he had to play us a tune before he left. When the tune ended, someone requested another tune. It was hilarious, as Joe's playing got faster and faster, in order to get the tune finished.

It was Christmas, and Joe, who stayed in a council house at Voeside, was making frequent visits to his neighbours. When my sister looked out the window, and saw Joe coming up the path yet again, she exploded: "Here comes Joe Smith again. Don't pour out any more whisky to him."

Joe found a chair and sat down in the kitchen.

"Wid do leck a cup o' tae Joe?"

"Yis, dat wid be fine dear."

"Whit does do tak in de tae Joe?"

"A peerie drap o'whisky dear."

Then there was the Sunday afternoon musical session in the lounge bar at Maryfield Hotel. Joe was in good fettle and was playing with gusto for the benefit of two American lady tourists. When he took a pause, one of them asked:

"What's the name of that tune, Mr Smith?"

"Well actually it's Kell an knocked corn. But to you dear, that would probably be: Cabbage and bruised oats."

Joe Smith and Basil Leask.

Shetland had a thriving dog fishing industry for some years from 1957 onwards. The dog fish were gutted and skinned at a Lerwick factory and the offal and rejects were added to the variety at Heogan. Dogfish livers were delivered in barrels and cooked in two specially adapted tanks which was my duty. After being boiled for the allotted time, the oil was skimmed off and put into steel drums. I often wondered if the oil ended up as cod liver oil capsules.

Dogfish gave off strong ammonia fumes during processing, making working conditions in the factory very unpleasant. I was almost overcome by the fumes while closing a steam valve to a tank which had erupted. Dog fish was a low grade product and difficult to process. The installation of a special hydraulic press was considered, and in that event, I would have been sent to Norway for training. The proposal was dropped, however, and I had to wait some years for the opportunity to see Norway.

6

THE 1960s – PART ONE

WHEN the contract with HIB ended in 1960, production at Heogan once more took a severe downturn and the workforce was cut back to one shift.

Jamie Henry left Heogan to work in Lerwick in 1960, and I was promoted to foreman. With only a handful of people employed, one simply mucked in wherever necessary.

One day Heckie Macdonald and I were repairing a broken chain in the fish conveyor I sent him to fetch some tools and, on his return, asked him to fetch a pair of pliers.

"What you need Tulloch, is little a black boy."

"No Hector, I don't need a little black boy when I have you."

As he went to fetch the pliers, I saw his shoulders shaking. Heckie enjoyed the fun just as much as I did.

In his young days, Heckie went to the drift net herring fishing.

He spoke of one particularly bad season at Yarmouth, when little herring was caught. Heckie got severe toothache, and had to get the tooth extracted. Having no money, he borrowed two shillings and sixpence from the skipper to pay the dentist. At the end of the season, his earnings only just covered the cost of extracting the tooth.

In the early 1960s a slump in the white fish market led to the unbelievable situation where the bulk of the Shetland

Heckie Macdonald, Bressay.

fleet, simply fished prime edible fish for fishmeal. This went against the grain with Robbie Williamson, skipper of the Whalsay boat *Unity*. Robbie found a spot where cruners were prolific, and landed his catch of inedible species from there on a daily bases. That area of seabed would thereafter be known as 'The Unity's Hol'.

Donald Manson deep in prime haddock.

Following a seal cull in Orkney in 1961, a small cargo boat laden with seal carcases berthed at the Heogan pier. We had been forewarned by the director in Aberdeen of the impending cargo. He had arranged that an attempt would be made to reduce the carcases to meal and oil.

To cut up a shipload of seal pups was a daunting task. Their big unseeing eyes seemed to stare back at you. It was the worst experience that I ever had at work, and I vowed that it would be the first and the last. The Heogan plant was not designed to process seal carcases, and the end product was of little value. The prospect of a second cargo was promptly ruled out.

Another low value product was crab shells, a waste product from a processing plant in Lerwick. Several loads were collected by *Jeannie* each week. The shells were processed in the usual manner, but the grinding/bagging area became an unhealthy workplace in the dust filled atmosphere. Breathing normally was impossible, as the fine dust got into the lungs.

In addition to tending the flame drier, I took on the duty of filling the bags. Holding my breath, I ran into the bagging area, removed the bag, went out for fresh air, and then returned to put another bag on the machine. Dovie would weigh and sew the bags when the dust settled.

Apart from being a low value product, the crab shells were tough on the machinery. When the cooker rotor sheared off, I repaired it in situ - but that incident put an end to crab shell processing at Heogan.

Christmas Day had always been a recognised holiday at Heogan. In mid-December 1960, however, we were told that in order to keep in line with the Fraserburgh factory, Christmas Day would be a normal working day. There was no way that I was going to do routine maintenance on Christmas Day, and the matter was dropped. At knock off time on Christmas Eve, Davie White appeared with a bottle of White Horse whisky to give us all a dram. After completing his round, Davie came back to Dovie: "Wid do lik anidder een Dovie?"

A smile spread over Dovie's face: "Oh I don't mind Davie, if you've got plenty to spare."

In September 1962 I bought a 'Standard' van in Aberdeen and kitted it out with mattress, sleeping bag and a few cooking utensils. As it was my first attempt at driving on the mainland, I did not linger in the Aberdeen traffic longer than necessary. I visited family in Cumnock, and friends in Aboyne, Brechin, the Isle of Skye and other locations.

Some days I lived rough, cooking on a gas ring and sleeping in the van. One night my overnight parking was in a disused quarry. As dawn broke, a fine waterfall caught my eye. With not a soul in sight, I stripped and took an ice cold shower beneath the waterfall. As it was then September, it was getting a bit chilly in the van at night. The 1,700 mile trip was, however, a memorable experience.

Before the days of Ro-Ro car ferries, getting a car on to the island of Bressay was no simple task. One option was to drive onto planks across the stern of the *Brenda*; the other was to drive on to planks across the deck of the *Jeannie*. I chose the latter as it was more convenient. Great improvement was made to this precarious method of transport in 1966, when HBP bought a boat complete with hydraulic lifting gear.

There had been five Up Helly Aa festivals in Bressay during the 1930s, but the festival was discontinued prior to the outbreak of war. Incidentally, Charlie Johnston, who was manager at Heogan in the years 1922-1939, was Bressay's first Jarl.

The idea of reviving the festival was fostered by Willie Johnny Kirkpatrick at a function in the Bressay hall in the autumn of 1961. A committee was formed, and the committee members became the Jarl's squad for 1962. Our Guizer Jarl was an Orcadian, James Lennie Matches. He was church missionary in Bressay at the time. Andrew White, the factory manager at Heogan, was appointed secretary and did the job with great enthusiasm. He and I made a house to house collection to raise money for the festival and complimentary tickets were given in return.

During the winter, the meal store at Heogan was made available for the Galley building. Chief Galley builders were my uncle, Harry Tulloch, and Robbie Anderson from Sullom. The torches were also made at Heogan, using an available supply of empty fish meal bags.

Laurence Anderson was asked to write the first Up Helly Aa Bill and went on to do the job admirably for many years His quick wit and choice of phrase regarding local episodes made hilarious reading and were invaluable in lightening up the festival. For some strange reason, I invariably did something during the course of the year to warrant a mention on the bill. One year, when my name didn't appear on the bill, I enquired what harm I had done. It was all good clean fun and few people took offence. The revival of Up Helly Aa went very well. It is still going strong, with the original Galley making a yearly appearance, fifty years on.

I was persuaded to be Jarl for1963. Unfortunately Davy White, our oil man at Heogan, died just days before the festival. The committee decided that the event should be cancelled, as a mark of respect, but the White family were adamant that the festival should go on as planned. Davy had been a fine man and a good workmate. I have many pleasant memories of him.

By 1963, production at Heogan had dropped to an all-time low, whereas the Fraserburgh factory was going flat out. I applied for a transfer, and on 10th January 1964, having no intention of returning to Heogan, packed some essentials into my van and headed for Fraserburgh.

Sandy Cardno, my old friend from 1955, arranged lodgings for me with his mother, Ruby Cardno, a fine old lady.

When I drove through the factory gates I could hardly believe my eyes, there were sprats everywhere. The pits were full to the brim, and sprats had been tipped onto the surrounding concrete yard. An old tractor with front loader attached stood there, lacking a driver. Without instruction, I started to clean up the overspill.

From the corner of my eye, I spotted a man in a brown work-coat approaching. It was Joe Campbell, the manager. "What are you doing?" was his greeting.

"Well, you can see what I'm doing," I answered.

"But anybody can do that."

I agreed that there was no question about that.

"But you can weld, can't you?"

"Yes, I have done some welding."

"Come with me, I have a wee job for you."

After that rather strange introduction, we got on well together. Joe, like me, was always trying to find a better way of doing things. I was never back on the tractor again, or expected to be involved in the production. Joe would dream up a new idea, and I was set to work.

Joe Campbell, manager at Fraserburgh, in 1964.

His greeting one morning was: "I have a wee job for you on the lathe today."

Confessing that I had never worked on a lathe, I was assured that I was not too old to learn. Then there was the day of his diplomatic approach: "We're affie pushed today, I wonder if you would mind helping us to load this lorry with meal?" It was hilarious, being asked so diplomatically, and I burst out laughing. But Joe was dead serious: "I know, I know. If I had been buggered about the way you have since you came here, I would tell the man where to go."

Joe had been involved at Heogan in a technical capacity in the past. He spoke of staying in the manager's house, where, I believe, his eldest daughter was born. I got to know and respect Joe during the four months that I worked at the Fraserburgh factory in 1964.

I never met Sigfinn Bartz-Johannessen, the company founder. He was highly spoken of by the older employees at Fraserburgh. When Sigfinn came on a visit, his first stop was always the meal store, where he weighed himself on the scales. He then went on a tour of the factory, stopping to shake hands with each employee in turn.

In Norway, fish processing on Stord came to an end in 1960 when Sigfinn decided to move on. Some of the processing machinery was moved to his factory at Knarrevik on the island of Sotra. A new company, Stord Bartz Industri A/S, was formed. They established an engineering works on the site of the old fishmeal and oil factory at Stord. Design, development and administration were done in Bergen, at the offices of Bergen Bartz A/S.

Sigfinn's aim was to design and produce more advanced fish processing machinery, and to diversify in other directions. His foresight led to the development of sugar presses and rotodisk driers. The driers found a lucrative market in the whisky distilling industry, where spent malt barley was dried and used as animal feed. Stord Bartz Industri machinery was first rate, and was marketed worldwide.

Fraserburgh factory, 1964.   *Bartz-Johannessen*

The Fraserburgh factory became a testing ground for the new machinery manufactured by Stord Bartz Industry. It could not have been easy for Joe Campbell to keep production going, with never-ending experiments going on and prototype machinery being installed – often to be thrown out again. His years as manager can only be described as a time of constant change and disruption.

After a hard week's work of 12 hour shifts at Fraserburgh, Saturday nights were a time to relax and have a dram. The local pubs were rated for the quality of their coffee. I thought it rather odd when someone said:

"You should go to Hotel such & such; their bar serves the best coffee in town." I soon to discovered that the coffee 'additive' was a good lashing of black rum.

The factory worked round the clock, two 12 hour shifts rotating each week. Production stopped at 6pm on Saturday, and commenced again at 6am on Sunday. One Saturday, just as the plant was being shut down for the night, the chains on the fish intake conveyor broke. I was surprised to see that no attempt was being made to do the repairs, and asked Joe Campbell Junior who was assistant manager: "Is no one going to fix that conveyor?"

"Do you know what night this is?"

"Yes, it's Saturday."

"Nobody is going to work here on a Saturday night," he said.

"Well, find someone to help me and I'll fix it."

He looked at me as if I had just landed from another planet. "Do you really mean that?"

"Saturday night is no more special to me than any other night Joe. I can have a dram any night, if I want to. It doesn't have to be Saturday." He gave me another strange look, shook his head, and walked away. A few minutes later, he was back.

"I've found a young fellow who is willing to help you, that is, if you really want to do this job." The repairs were duly done, and the factory was back in production at six on Sunday morning.

One night when things were quiet, I took my van into the factory to do an under seal. Jacking it up, I put on my oilskins and, using a steam hose, did a thorough cleaning job. A mixture of grease and fish oil was applied with a paint brush when the metal dried.

There was a nasty smell of burning fish oil from the exhaust for a few days, but when dust and road grit was added, it became an excellent under seal, and was never touched by me again.

Some time later, I traded in the vehicle at Westshore garage in Scalloway. Hearing on the grapevine that they had steam-cleaned the van, I found an excuse to call in at the garage. When met by the mechanic who had obviously done the clean-up, he asked just what on earth I had used as an under seal? Enquiring how it had stood up, he answered: "Man, sho wis just shining."

In late April 1964, Joe delivered an unwelcome message. "George Reid has been through from Aberdeen. He wants you to go back to Bressay, at least for the summer season."

I thought about it for a moment before replying, "All right I'll go, but if things don't work out, will you give me a job back here?"

"You will get a job from me any day, laddie," was the reassuring answer. And so, with some apprehension, it was back to Heogan again.

Returning home, I had three second hand black and white TV sets for the family packed into my van. We were about to get a TV mast on the Wart of Bressay, which would send a black and white signal from the BBC for a few hours viewing each evening.

Upon returning to Heogan on 17 May 1964, Andrew White was on sick leave and in his absence, I had to take charge. In early August, director George Reid came on a visit. After a tour of the factory, he asked if I would take over as manager. I declined, saying that I had no qualifications to do such a job.

"I think you are capable," he said. "If you accept the responsibility, I will be behind you, and if you make a mistake, just tell me, and I will stand by you."

After some thought, I accepted the challenge, and never forgot those kind words of assurance. One day I made a wrong decision and picked up the phone to confess. George was a man of his word: "Just put it down to experience," he said.

I was to gain a lot of experience in the next 22 years.

George Reid had been a company director since 1946, and became managing director in 1965. He therefore had first-hand knowledge of all aspects of the company. During his frequent visits to Heogan the procedure was to go on a tour of the site, from the pier to the meal store.

George had good mechanical knowledge. He always remembered if there had been a breakdown on a certain machine, and would enquire if it had given more trouble since his last visit.

I soon learned when it was appropriate to request any capital expenditure; it had to be when the pits were full of fish, with the factory going flat out. His conservative thinking, and at times lack of foresight, was a drawback, however. Once, when I was putting up an argument for a workers' pay rise, he asked: "Does everyone have to get this pay rise?"

"Of course, you cannot give an increase to some and not to others."

"Surely not the woman," he said.

That didn't deserve an answer. I just saw to it, that 'the woman' got a pay rise like everyone else.

It was sometimes a balancing act to get a fair deal for the workers and, at the same time, act in the company's best interest. In spite of his conservative thinking, George was an honest man who would never cheat anyone. The company was his life. He had no hobbies, saying that he would never retire. He liked to relax with a dram, when work was done.

With a change of management in 1964, the factory got an almost new workforce. Dovie Linklater went on sick leave in January 1964, and was unable to return to work. Ronald Birnie left in June 1964 to join the Lighthouse service, where he spent the rest of his working life. The McDonalds and Whites moved to Edinburgh in November 1965. Andrew Tulloch left in July1967 to find work in Edinburgh.

Ronald Birnie in 2006.

I contacted Jamie Henry asking him to come back in his former capacity as foreman, and was delighted when he accepted. Jamie returned on 19th November 1964. He became a great support to me, and together we were able to start making changes for the better.

One of the first jobs was to fill that useless settling hole in the pits, where 'Dutchie' had taken a plunge in 1955. It had never served any useful purpose in my time at Heogan. Thereafter, there were always improvements to be made, and the job became quite challenging. In order to get to grips with the system, I did the office work from September 1964 till May 1965, but I realised that I was wasting time. Laurence Anderson, who had done the office work at Heogan in the mid-1950s and 1960s was asked to do the books in the evenings. The arrangement worked well, greatly reducing my workload. Laurence took care of the books until May 1967, when my wife took over the duties.

When Jamie Henry returned to Heogan in 1964, he worked initially as shift foreman and in 1968 formed our construction gang. Jamie was a good leader, well liked and respected. He would set the pace, and never expected more of others than he was prepared to do himself.

Members of the construction gang were, in the main, Bressay men, including Bertie Birnie, Robbie Eunson, Harry Tulloch, James John Tulloch, Jamie Deyell, Charlie Henry and George Peattie.

Laurence Anderson, Bressay

They did much good work in developing the site over a period of six years. The team was disbanded in 1973, when Jamie chose a less strenuous job as store man for P&O Ferries in Lerwick. He worked there until retiring age in 1985.

Bertie Birnie started work at Heogan on 27 July 1965, and worked there until he retired on his 65th birthday on 27 November 1986. He was a good all-rounder, reliable and trustworthy. Initially, he worked as pier man and later became part of the construction gang. As a young man, Bertie served in the RAF. He was posted to Sullom Voe, where he spent most of the war years. He had many stories to tell, but got a lot of work done 'between stories'.

Harry Tulloch and his granddaughter, Fiona, 1960s.

Bertie Birnie.   *George Birnie*

THE 1960S – PART TWO

IN MARCH 1965, George Reid organised a trip for Joe Campbell (junior) and me to visit the parent company in Bergen, Norway. As George put it: "It will widen your horizon."

Joe had been assistant manager at Fraserburgh for some time. It was assumed that he would eventually follow in his father's footsteps as factory manager.

The ten day trip was an unforgettable experience, and my horizon became wider than bargained for. The flight to Bergen was not as the crow flies. We flew half way around Europe to get there. George Reid accompanied us, staying three days in order to attend a board meeting.

Christian Bartz-Johannessen had taken over from his father, Sigfinn, and was by then the principle shareholder of HBP. We had met previously on his visits to Shetland. Christian loved Shetland and made many trips across the North Sea over the years. He was a kind and honest man whose quick wit and sense of humour often led to hilarious situations.

We were invited to his home in Bergen, where we spent a pleasant evening with him and his family. For the following evening, he had booked a table at Belevue, a spectacular restaurant situated on the mountain side with a magnificent view over Bergen. The food was excellent. I had a steak, and remember that George Reid was persuaded by Christian to order

Joe Campbell Jnr., Assistant Manager at Fraserburgh.

cod tongues (considered to be a delicacy in Norway). George was nibbling at his plateful of cod tongues, making no comment until Christian asked: "What do you think of the cod tongues, George?"

"Mm, interesting," was the diplomatic reply.

Our accommodation was at the Orion hotel which, at the time, was considered one of the best in Bergen. A huge log fire and live piano music in the lounge bar area created a cosy atmosphere. Great food was served, and the huge, self-service breakfast spread was definitely sufficient to keep one going all day. Our rooms were very comfortable. Joe's had a great view of the harbour, and mine, a breath-taking view of the snow covered mountains and the terraced houses built into the mountain side. I fell for the place there and then. Even today, when in Bergen, I feel as if I have come home.

We spent the first three days at the company's large office, where engineers, draftsmen, technicians and administrators made up a workforce of about seventy employees. I had already met some of the engineers on their visits to Heogan and it was good to meet them again. This was my first of many trips to the Bergen office.

The original fish meal and oil factory at Stord had got a change of use and a new name, 'Stord Bartz Industri A.S'. It had been developed into an engineering works, where fish processing machinery was produced for sale worldwide. Design and development was done in the Bergen office under the name of 'Bergen Bartz', hence the large number of employees.

Christian owned a fish meal and oil factory at Knarrevik on the island of Sotra. One day he brought us there in his car to see the factory. I always welcomed the opportunity to see other factories, as no two are alike. After an interesting tour of the factory, and meeting the workers, we were about to get back into Christian's car, when he spotted a coil of wire mesh netting.

"That's just what I need for my garden," he announced, as he grabbed the wire and attempted, without success, to stow it in the boot of his car.

I saw the solution and advised: "If you take out the spare wheel, you will find room for the wire, and you can stow the spare wheel on top."

This duly done, Christian turned to me with a grin and exclaimed: "You're not as stupid as you look."

Several years later, I figured out what he really meant, and that he had actually paid me a compliment. He had obviously been thinking in Norwegian,"Du er ikke så dum som du ser ut," (there's more to you than meets the eye). Direct translation can sometimes backfire.

Christian thought it would be an interesting experience for Joe and me to go skiing on the mountains above Bergen. With great enthusiasm he arranged fitting us out from a stock of skis, sticks and boots. Finding boots to fit Joe was easy; but my big feet presented a problem. Christian came to check on progress: "Let me see that foot of yours."

I held up my foot. He took a quick look at it, then shaking his head exclaimed: "I don't think *you* need skis!"

When at last suitable boots were found we embarked upon a new adventure. Two young engineers, Bjørn Skulstad and Jan Olsen, were appointed as our instructors. They had a lot of fun watching our first, feeble attempts at standing upright on skis.

Eventually I got my balance, and was off downhill at good speed, but trouble lay ahead when a tree appeared, directly in my path. I tried to take evasive action, but to no avail, ending up with a ski at either side of the tree. Luckily it was only a small tree, and no real damage was done.

The scene from the mountain overlooking Bergen was fantastic, and I was hooked, vowing that someday I would return.

On 29th March, Joe, Mike Rogers and I met in the bar of the Orion Hotel. Mike was an English car salesman that Joe and I had met some days earlier. He was staying long term at our hotel. While having a dram, we were enjoying the cosy scene of a roaring log fire with soothing live piano music in the background. My 30th birthday had been, and gone, three days earlier. Suddenly, Joe asked: "What would you like to do to celebrate your birthday?"

"Well, a night out with a Norwegian girl would do for a start."

I had noticed some pretty girls in Bergen.

Joe again: "Why don't we go out to celebrate?"

And so, with no further ado, we set out to explore Bergen's night life.

Mike, with his local knowledge, was appointed guide. After some exploring, we arrived at a restaurant with a dance floor, where live music was in full swing. And there, my horizon widened considerably, as I set eyes on my future wife for the first time.

Picking up courage, I asked her to dance. When the music turned into a twist I was horrified, but somehow got through it. Luckily my dance partner spoke English, which was a bonus, as I could not speak a word of Norwegian at the time – my Shetland dialect adding to the confusion.

She said that her name was Bjarnhild, and that she was working as a stewardess on M.V. *Harald Jarl*, one of the 'Hurtigruten' ships sailing the eleven day round trip, Bergen-Kirkenes-Bergen.

We had several dances together and as the dancing came to an end, I ordered a taxi for Bjarnhild and her two female companions and accompanied them to the pier where the ship was berthed. As strangers were not allowed on board, we stood talking for some time. Bjarnhild told me that her home town was Kirkenes, situated at 70° north, almost at the Russian border and well beyond the Arctic Circle. I got very interested, as the Arctic has always held a fascination for me.

On the spur of the moment I asked: "Will you join me for a meal tomorrow evening?"

"I don't know if I can, as we are sailing at 10pm and we are not allowed to go ashore on the night of departure from Bergen."

I must have looked disappointed because she added: "If I can manage to get away, I will come."

And so we agreed that if possible, we would meet at 6.30 pm.

Next morning, when Joe and I reported at the office, I was in for a shock when Christian announced his plans for the day: "I have arranged for you to visit Stord today to see the engineering works where we manufacture processing machinery. The journey by road and ferry takes some time, so you won't be back until late tonight."

"Oh good God" I exclaimed, thinking of my dinner date.

"Why? Did you want to be back early tonight?" Christian was quick off the mark, looking at me inquiringly: "Well, yes, if it is possible."

Christian made no comment, but rose from his seat and shot out the door. Minutes later he was back with a grin on his face: "That's all right. I've chartered a small sea plane to fly you there and back."

I was thunderstruck to think that he would do such a thing without hesitation. Soon the sea plane was alongside, and within minutes we were airborne. The aerial view of mountains, rivers, lochs and small townships was spectacular. Turning to my companion I remarked: "There's only one engine on this plane Joe, I hope it doesn't stop."

"Don't you start; it's bad enough sitting here without your comments." Only then did I realise that he was terrified, holding on so tight that his knuckles were white.

We were on a guided tour of the works, when a man came to inform us that our plane had got a technical problem: "It is no problem" he said "The seaplane that delivers the mail will take you back to Bergen".

Joe looked briefly skywards before turning to me as he exploded: "That's done it. There's no way you're going to get me up there again in one of these damned things."

Joe made his return journey to Bergen as originally planned, by sea and road.

Our dinner date was much too short, but we kept in touch by letter and phone. In August 1965, Bjarnhild set foot on Shetland for the first time; she arrived here exhausted, after a tough season on *Harald Jarl*. Four weeks later, I accompanied her back to Norway.

We went to visit her sister on the island of Nøtterøy in southern Norway, where for three days, I didn't understand a word. Our next stop was in Trondheim, where I hired a car, driving on the right for the first time. Navigating a roundabout in the opposite direction was a bit confusing.

At Trondheim I met Dag and Rune, Bjarnhild's two sons from a former marriage. She had a full time job translating, as each time I opened my mouth, one of them would immediately ask: "What's he saying Mama?" It was mutual however, as I had no idea what they were saying either. After a memorable two weeks in Norway, it was back to the grind at Heogan once more.

When Christian came on a visit to Heogan in the autumn of 1965, he commented: "I hear you are planning to get married."

"Yes, that's right."

"Have you set the date?"

"Yes, we are planning for a January wedding."

"Do you think that's wise?" he asked, with a twinkle in his eye.

Not sure where he was coming from, I asked what he meant.

"Well she's from the north isn't she? You know, the people up there go to sleep for the winter. If I were you, I would wait until spring; there may be more life in her by then."

He was full of fun, and could find the most hilarious things to say at the spur of the moment.

We were married in the Bressay church and celebrated our wedding in traditional Shetland style, with 120 guests in the local hall. Unfortunately, none of Bjarnhild's family and friends were able to attend. Travelling the long distance in mid-winter was a much greater deterrent then than it is today.

It took Bjarnhild some time to figure out who had been at our wedding, but mother's guest list in our wedding album became an invaluable reference.

Only days after our wedding, Bjarnhild and I were at the British Legion to celebrate Up Helly Aa 1966. Bjarnhild was intrigued when a squad of polar bears walked through the door. Following their act, their requested dance was a Norwegian waltz and one very tall polar bear invited her to dance. When masks were removed, the bear was none other than Magnus Shearer.

Our wedding on 20ᵗʰ January, 1966.   *Dennis Coutts*

We were pleasantly surprised to get a visit from Magnus on his 50ᵗʰ birthday. He had become interested in building a house on Bressay and was looking for a site. The following year we were delighted to have him and Maisie as our nearest neighbours. Our friendship grew and we spent many pleasant evenings in their company.

Magnus had many roles in his service to the Shetland Community. Having served in the Royal Navy during WWII, he was secretary for the RNLI, Chairman for the Fishermen's Mission, Swedish and German consul, and in later years Lord Lieutenant for Shetland.

Things were starting to look up at Heogan in 1966 and it was possible to employ more workers. Among them were two local handymen; my uncle, Harry Tulloch, and James John Tulloch. They were given the task of refurbishing the manager's house. It had been many years since a family lived there. The handymen also converted an old hut into a fine office and lab. We stayed three months with my parents at East Ham, before moving to the manager's house at Heogan in April 1966. It would be our home for the next five years.

Bjarnhild went to Norway in June to fetch Dag and Rune, and I drove to Newcastle to meet them in a hired a car. Her father also came to visit us for the first time. Bjarnhild had a full time job as translator, but children learn fast. The boys were speaking English long before I could converse in Norwegian. When I made a feeble attempt, they would promptly answer in English.

Our first Christmas living as a family at Heogan was in 1966. Christmas Eve was celebrated in traditional Norwegian style as a family occasion. Bjarnhild did much preparation beforehand with home bakes sufficient to feed an army. It became a tradition that my parents, aunts, uncles, my sister and brother in law all celebrated Christmas Eve with us, Norwegian style.

The afternoons, during the years we stayed at Heogan, were reserved for the workers. They were all invited into our house for a dram, followed by tea or coffee, home baked bannocks and reisted mutton. Bjarnhild also introduced home-made 'sursild' (pickled herring) as an additive to the open sandwiches, which became a very popular choice. Half bottles would appear like magic, followed by a fiddle, and in no time, a party would be going full swing.

With the passage of time, the workforce increased to the extent that there was hardly room to move in the small house. One member of the construction gang stumbled and crashed into the corner on top of our Christmas tree. Thereafter he became known as 'the lumberjack'.

No work of any consequence was ever done on Christmas Eve, so it became logical to declare the day a holiday. For some years a lively Christmas party was held in the Lerwick hotel, with dancing to the music of Jim Halcrow's band. By 1974, with the provision of a new canteen, we celebrated our annual Christmas party on the last working day of the year. My contribution was to get up very early to roast the huge turkey, packed with oat meal stuffing, in time for the dinner party at 12 noon. The two cooks completed all the necessary preparations for a great social event.

Fish intake at the factory in 1965 was only 2,264 tons, but in spite of that there was a degree of optimism at a higher level – and slowly, the development began. A new and much needed meal store was erected on a site near the Fresher's pier. The new building was portal frame, clad in corrugated cement-asbestos sheeting. A positive displacement blower, complete with some 100 metres of 5 inch pipeline, conveyed the meal from the grinding area to the bagging point in the new meal store.

Some necessary repairs were done to the piers and buildings, while the eight oil storage tanks, referred to earlier, were cleaned and tarred; thereafter the chipping hammers became relics of the past.

Boat builder Jamie Smith was commissioned to build a 21ft Shetland model boat powered by a 1½ hp Stuart Turner engine. Small gauge railway lines were secured to an existing slipway. With a cradle to suit the boat and assisted by an old hand winch, taking the boat ashore was a simple task. The boat was open, and I frequently got very wet when the sea was choppy in the north harbour.

One beautiful calm winters evening I left the boat tied up the factory pier,

Andrew Tulloch, 1965.

MV Jeannie *with new grab, 1966.*

and, before going to bed, went to check that it was secure. My vision of the boat was unclear in the dim light. Shaking my head I thought: "What's wrong with my eyesight?"

It eventually dawned on me that I was looking through water. With the rising tide, the boat had come up under a vertical fender and sunk. As it now had to be taken ashore, the time was appropriate for my uncle Harry to build a cabin on it. Following that, I could cross the harbour in comfort.

The grab.

My cousin Ray Tulloch joined the workforce in July 1965, and became a great asset to the company. His first job was as truck driver, collecting offal from filleting factories in Lerwick and Scalloway for delivery to the *Jeannie*. We had procured a truck with a hydraulic operated tail platform for the purpose. (Another cast off from Fraserburgh).But the vehicle was in good condition, and served the purpose for several years.

When Ray was promoted to foreman in August 1966, Donald Manson became the truck driver. The factory was again working double shifts for the first time since the late 1950s. Sprats were caught for the first time in Shetland waters during 1966 but it never developed on a scale to match landings at Fraserburgh and other ports on the North East coast at that time. Sprat landings amounted to only 1700 tons that year. Foreign vessels made their first landings in 1967 when production rose to 9,267 tons for that year.

By 1966 the old *Jeannie* that had served so well, came to the end of her working days; she was taken ashore in Leirness Voe, and was eventually broken up.

Jeannie's replacement was MV *Shanty*, a 52ft timber boat, described in the Norwegian translated ships papers as, 'made of tree'. The *Shanty* had been used as a small freight carrier in Norway. She was powered by a single cylinder Wickman engine, referred to in Shetland as a 'bung bung'. Complete with hydraulic winch and a grab, she was an ideal flitboat, serving us well until the arrival of the first Bressay car ferry, MV *Grima*, in October 1975.

Shearers yard with Jeannie *alongside.*   *Magnus Shearer*

Jimbo Clark on Bressay Up Helly Aa Day, 1962.

Loading the Shanty *at Symbister.*

Tied up at Symbister.

During her nine years' service, *Shanty* transported thousands of tons of fish offal, and all sorts of building material across the harbour. Transport of cars and tractors was now simple, as they were lifted on board. Purpose-made spreader bars and wheel nets ensured that cars were undamaged while being lifted. She also served as a ferry, collecting workers from Lerwick on a daily basis, and dockers when required to load meal boats. *Shanty's* first crew was Jimbo Clark and Leonard Scollay.

Jimbo had done his 'sea time' crossing Bressay Sound as skipper of the ferry *Brenda*, and Leonard had skippered the pilot boat *Budding Rose* for some years.

Shanty's workload became overstretched when four new filleting factories were built on Whalsay, Skerries and Yell. A second boat was purchased from Skerries. She was the ex-fishing boat *St Clair* LK250, and renamed *Valorous*. The original *Valorous* had been the flitboat in use in the 1950s. The new *Valorous* was converted to a flitboat, with adapted steel lined hold, hydraulic winch and fish grab, plus a general purpose grab. Her skipper was Billy Clark. She was a good sea boat, giving good service until she was sold in 1975, with the arrival of inter-island car ferries.

8

THE 1960s – PART THREE

RAY was promoted to assistant manager in August 1967 and later, as was done at Fraserburgh, we worked as joint managers for a time. It was an unsatisfactory arrangement, and when he got an opportunity in 1977, Ray left Heogan to join the crew of the Bressay ferry, MV *Grima*. He was soon promoted to skipper, and worked in that capacity until he retired in September 2000.

Ray had played pranks all his life, going to endless bother to set the scene. Therefore, it was no surprise to hear what he got up to at Heogan, even when he should have been setting a better example.

We had got a new bird scarer at the factory, but that device was to scare more than the birds. It was a gas operated cannon, and the word cannon was appropriate. One day, Ray put the cannon and gas bottle in a wheel barrow, covering it with meal bags. He then set the mechanism on two minutes delay and instructed Graham Henderson to wheel the barrow from the factory to the

Ray Tulloch at the wheel of the MV Grima, *1980.*

Bertie Birnie and Graham Henderson on the ferry Norna.

Freshers pier. When his hidden cargo exploded, one can imagine Graham's reaction.

The downside of living so close to the factory was that the work was never ending. With production problems in the factory and the ever increasing development around us, it was impossible to have a day off and just be home with the family.

One Saturday afternoon when things got out of hand, I walked in the door saying to Bjarnhild: "Throw some things into a suitcase; we're going on the boat tonight."

"Are you crazy?" she retorted.

"Not yet, but if we don't get out of here *now*, I will be."

And so I made three phone calls, first to my mother, asking her to look after the boys for a few days; the next was to my assistant Ray Tulloch, to tell him that we were going for a break; the third call was to the director in Aberdeen. By 5pm we were on *St Clair,* heading south – our quickest exit ever. After a few days driving in a hired car in 'Bonnie Scotland', we returned home, refreshed and able to carry on once more. We realised, however, that we could not stay at Heogan indefinitely.

During our early years as a family, we bought four pair of skies in Norway. At that time, Shetland got much more snow in winter than we do today. It was not uncommon for the roads to be blocked for days on end. Bjarnhild had grown up in arctic Norway. Snow and skiing was therefore second nature to her. The boys were also excellent skiers and never missed an opportunity to use their skies. To the great entertainment of the factory workers, the boys collected a pile of fish boxes and building them up high, made a ski jump, where they flew over at great speed. Bjarnhild and the boys had slalom skies, whereas mine were lightweight cross country skies. I could move from A to B, but never became a good skier.

In 1967 a new meal store was built (now used as a workshop) by the combined effort of our workforce and three hired bricklayers. This was the year when a golden opportunity for development at Heogan was looming, with huge supplies of raw material on our doorstep. Norwegian purse net boats were congregating in droves in Lerwick. On one occasion, I counted 50 Norwegian boats, either moored at the piers in Lerwick, or lying at anchor in the harbour.

The Norwegian fleet, 1965.   *Dennis Coutts*

In the early days of purse seine fishing, a dory was required to assist closing the net. These small dories could not operate with wind speeds exceeding force five; consequently, when the wind blew, as it often does in a Shetland summer, the fleet came in to shelter. Word spread that there was a fish meal and oil factory on Bressay, and boats were soon queuing up to deliver small quantities of 20 to 50 tonnes, before going back to sea.

Willie Gordon was another Bressay character, who worked in the pits. No sooner had he got the pits empty and washed, when more Norwegian boats arrived, filling the pits to the brim again. One day in sheer exasperation Willie exploded: "Why to hell can't these foreigners go home to their own country with their fish?"

At that time, most of the Norwegian pursers carried a grab. As we had no facilities to discharge them, they used their own grabs. Neither did we have any means of measuring quantities delivered; it was done more or less by estimate and trust.

This haphazard way of working was unacceptable to all, and an 'Iris' fish discharging machine was bought from Denmark. The machine was mobile and quite versatile, and could be used on any type, or size of boat.

Harry Hunter at home.

I have no idea who dreamt up the Shetland by-name for the machine, but a fisherman referred to it as 'Da Gleppie' and the name stuck. These machines were to be the standard method of discharging boats at Heogan for the next 25 years. With the new discharging machinery in place, fish deliveries were measured by volume, using a mechanical hectolitre measure, as was standard practice in Norway. Manning the machines on the pier was an exacting job, calling for a competent and trustworthy man. His duty was to ensure that each drum was full as it passed beneath the hopper. Failing to do so was costly for the company, and good for the fishermen.

An abundant supply of first class raw material was now available. Production during 1967 had increased to 9,267 tons, of which 5,073 tons were from foreign boats. Now, for the first time in 10 years, it was necessary for the factory to work round the clock. I contacted a few locals like Harry Hunter, George Williamson, Willie Manson, Magnie Tulloch and others, arranging for them to work nightshift as and when required.

The arrangement worked well, as they all had daytime work to attend to. They were happy to earn the extra money and I suppose it was a tempting challenge. They were, however, deprived of sleep and at times it showed. Harry Hunter was one that seemed to be able to go for days on end without sleep. I was constantly telling him that he was pushing himself too hard. One night when he arrived to start work, I observed that he looked rested and said: "Well, you have had a sleep today."

"Yea," said Harry in his Unst dialect, "I hed twa oors."

The inefficient, worn out machinery was, however, an ongoing problem, and we were forever processing decaying fish. It was almost impossible to make a decent end product.

Jacob Bø from Askøy near Bergen was the company's engineer at that time. He and I were in agreement that a modern, well equipped factory should be built. The existing factory had stood on the site for some 70 years and due to the corrosive atmosphere, was showing its age.

Large modern factories had sprung up along the Norwegian coast to take advantage of the new development, and here we were, sitting right in the middle of rich fishing grounds with an outdated factory full of obsolete machinery. The choice of the factory site had been ideal at the outset, but things had moved on. The size of fishing boats was ever on the increase, and water depth at the pier was inadequate.

The board agreed that the time was right for investment, but decided to apply caution and develop slowly. One director's attitude was: "Let's just build from the profits."

And so a great opportunity was lost. The decision was taken to install one line of new machinery in the existing building. That proved to be a major operation with the heaviest item weighing 27 tonnes, and the wooden piers at Heogan incapable of carrying such a weight.

Jacob Bø was put in charge of planning the installation. He was a capable and pleasant man, well liked and respected. His father had been manager of a fish meal and oil factory in Norway, and Jacob, after a technical education, had followed in his father's footsteps.

He had managed factories in Chile and had some interesting stories to tell from his travels. Jacob spoke of a time when the Chilean fleet were not finding any fish, and the factories stood idle. He got the idea to charter a small plane to search for shoals of fish. The plane had only one engine, with a fuel tank on each wing. All was going well until the engine stopped. It was quickly discovered that a valve to one tank, had been closed by mistake. While the pilot tried start the engine, Jacob was frantically pumping with a hand pump to clear the airlock. To their great relief, the engine finally came to life when they were only metres above the waves.

Jacob was hard at it, planning the installation for 1968. His first priority was to design new 'fish storage bins', but the old name would never change, and the term pits remained. When the plans arrived by post, Jamie Henry and I studied them and were in agreement that it was just what was needed.

I handed the plans to Jamie asking: "Will you take on to build this, using direct labour?"

Jamie accepted the challenge and a first class job was done on time. This was just the start. Under Jamie's leadership, the team worked nonstop on construction for the next six years.

Responsibility and pressure of work was taking its toll, and I needed a break. In August 1967 we packed our Volkswagen Beetle, and the four of us set out for an extended holiday in Norway.

For me it was marvellous to get away, and for Bjarnhild and the boys, great to be back in their homeland again. We crossed the North Sea from Newcastle to Bergen on MV *Leda* and headed north – our destination Kirkenes, Bjarnhild's birth place. Overnight accommodation on the way north was, in the main, with family and friends.

I had an 8mm cine film camera and wanted to photograph everything I saw, so much so, that in frustration, Bjarnhild said: "If you stop at every bend in the road to take film, we will never get to Kirkenes."

After two weeks, we eventually got there. But for me it was an unforgettable experience. I still vividly remember the sight of the spectacular waterfalls in Hardanger. It had been raining heavily, and wherever we looked, a sea of water poured down from the mountains.

One memorable stop was in Honningsvåg, where we stayed with Bjarnhild's Aunt Margit. She was a real character, and full of stories. Unfortunately, at that time, my Norwegian vocabulary was still quite limited and once more Bjarnhild had to translate. When we met that charming old lady some years later, it was a pleasure to converse with her in her own language.

While staying in Honningsvåg, we drove to North Cape where it was bitterly cold for late August. I also visited two fish meal factories on the island. Our final destination was Kirkenes to visit Bjarnhild's father. Bjarne was delighted to see us all, and we spent an enjoyable six days in his company. As I had heard so much about the place where my wife grew up, it was of great interest to see Kirkenes for the first time. The town had been rebuilt following total destruction in World War II. Our stay in Kirkenes was all too short and I vowed to return again. I love the north as much as Bjarnhild does, and we have been back many times over the years.

We got out of Finnmark in the nick of time. Snow was in the air, and one week later the roads and mountain passes where we had driven, were blocked by snow.

The old Volkswagen Beetle had a full load to pull on the way south, including a lady passenger from Kirkenes, who decided that she would like to see Shetland. Dag and Rune were disgruntled at having to share the back seat with one large, very talkative female, but all went well. We drove through Finland and into Sweden where we visited friends, before heading back into Norway.

A new dining table was bought in Bergen, and secured on the roof rack, with boxes and suitcases piled high on top. Bjarnhild's enthusiasm for Norwegian food tends to get a bit out of hand, but it is amazing just how much can be packed into a small car. After the long and very enjoyable holiday, we arrived back at Heogan, refreshed and ready to start again.

9

THE 1960s – PART FOUR

PLANS for the installation of new machinery were now high profile. As no pier on the island was capable of supporting the weight of the new plant, it was decided that the slipway at Heogan would serve the purpose.

The Freshers pier was strengthened and upgraded, by adding a right angled extension to facilitate the oil tankers that would deliver fuel oil. Our construction gang ran concrete foundations for a 300 ton fuel oil tank on a site adjacent to the factory. Bertie Sutherland, a Bressay man, was contracted to construct a six inch pipeline from the pier to the tank site.

In January 1968 two fitter/welders, Åsmund Sandnes and Egil Nordhaug, arrived from Norway. Their job was to prepare the slipway for landing the new machinery. Good quality railway beams were welded together and secured to the slipway. They constructed a ramp from H-beams, designed to convert the angle of the slipway to horizontal. The ramp was designed to rest on the railway beams and to slide up or down the slipway to suit the tide.

A robust winch was found, lying dormant in Scalloway. Its owner was unwilling to sell, but agreed that we could borrow it, and so the old winch was refurbished and made as good as new. It was fitted with an electric motor with gearbox and placed on a substantial foundation,

Shanty *and* Budding Rose *standing by.*

some distance from the slipway. The shore facilities were then ready for use.

On a very cold and windy day in March 1968, a ship with heavy lifting gear dropped anchor in the north harbour. Her cargo was the long awaited new machinery. Some 36 hours later, the wind dropped, and as the ship was by then on demurrage (had used the allotted time), we took the decision to start at 11pm.

The first item over the side was a new boat, to replace the 21ft Shetland model. A robust, specially constructed steel raft with polystyrene flotation was the next item in the water. H-beams of equal gauge to that of the slipway ramp had been mounted on its deck. The first heavy lift to be taken ashore was the 18 tonne shell, or 'stator' of the Rotadisk drier. It was carefully placed on the raft and then towed to the slipway.

The raft ready to land new machinery.

Prior to each landing, Malakoff divers secured the ramp by chains to the railway lines, to suit the state of the tide. Johnnie Sinclair was the young diver. He told me recently that he got very cold, and remembers sitting in front of a roaring fire in our house, to thaw out between dives.

The new drier safely ashore.

The raft, on arrival at the slipway, was secured to the ramp and the slow operation of winching the machine ashore commenced. By using steel wire, with block and tackle via the winch, movement was reduced to a snail pace. The next item taken ashore was the drier rotor, placed on a cradle for stability. It was the heaviest item in the consignment, weighing 27 tonnes.

The 27 ton drier motor.

Two items had been collected at Renfrew, a Babcock & Wilcox oil fired boiler and an electric transformer. The latter was the last item to be transported on the raft. Landing it on the slip was the only mishap of the whole operation.

It toppled over, bursting a tube and spewing oil into the sea. Small items were transhipped to *Shanty* and freighted to the pier. After working 26 hours non-stop, we were all very cold and tired and relieved when the job was done.

When the machinery was all safely ashore I left Ray in charge, while Bjarnhild and I took a short break on mainland Scotland. On our return, the installation work was in full swing.

Safely on the ramp.

Installing the machinery was very labour intensive. A team of 18 Norwegian fitter/welders did the installation. Everything was done by hand tools, as neither crane nor forklift was available. Using tackle and jacks, things gradually took shape. The old factory was almost wrecked in the process of getting the machinery in place.

Steel plates for the construction of a 300 ton capacity fuel tank were included in the ship's cargo. A three man team of

The new press on slipway.

Norwegian welders soon had the tank constructed.Lodgings were found for the Norwegians in private houses throughout the island. They were a jolly, friendly lot and were well accepted on Bressay, so much so, that a party in their honour was organised in the local hall.

On 17th May, Norway's Independence Day, the Norwegians (with Bjarnhild's help) arranged a return party for the locals. Viktor Petersen, a very happy and likable fellow, was in good fettle and decided to make a speech. We waited in anticipation as his English was quite limited. There was a hushed silence as Viktor took the stage: "Ladies and gentlemen," he began. "You don't know me, but when I say thank you, then you know me very vell." That was the entire content of his speech, and the place erupted.

The months of construction were a lively time for us, living in the middle of the development. Heogan became a focal point on the island. Local men were employed at the factory earning good money, and there was a general feeling of optimism in the air.

We got to know Åsmund Sandnes well during the months of construction, and our friendship continued throughout his life. He was a very special person and had a great admiration for Shetland; so much so, that in retirement Åsmund and his wife Ada, were like migrating birds, returning to Shetland each spring.

As a young man, Åsmund, like many others fled Norway to take up the fight against German occupation of his country. He told us about being billeted in Skegness. When a request for volunteers to go to Shetland came up, Åsmund's hand immediately shot in the air. On arrival in Shetland he was delighted to discover that he was to serve with Leif Larsen on *Vigra*. She was one of the three sub-chasers gifted by the U.S. Navy as replacements for the lost Norwegian fishing boats of the Shetland Bus.

Engineer Jacob Dalland, an employee of Stord Bartz Industry, was appointed charge hand for the machinery installation. He had worked in America, and his accent and mannerisms showed through. He was immediately dubbed 'The Yank' by the Bressay boys who never missed an opportunity to tag a by-name. After some weeks, Jacob was called to another consignment and Knut Riise was appointed charge hand. Knut spoke in a very rough voice but he was popular and well respected. He was a good leader, and harmony prevailed.

Some time later, I heard of an episode in northern Norway, where Dalland and Riise were installing machinery in a factory. Dalland was called away to take care of a problem elsewhere. As he hurriedly left, he asked Riise to arrange for his toolkit to be sent to Bergen. Knut found a huge packing case which had been used to deliver an oil separator. He secured Jacobs tool box in one corner and in the opposite corner hung up his boiler suit on a nail. Knut addressed the box and dispatched it on a 1,000 mile sea journey to Bergen. When Jacobs's wife got a call from the shipping company to say that a consignment was waiting collection, she asked them to delivery it. On his homecoming, Jacob found the huge box in his garden, delivered by a crane truck.

Keeping production going while construction work was in progress was difficult, and it was a relief when the new plant was ready to go at midnight on a fine summer night in June 1968. I don't remember the date, and no longer have records, but what I do remember is that it was late on a Friday night when Jacob Bø asked: "Do you want to start tonight?"

Eager to see the new machinery in motion, I confirmed: "Of course I do."

"I have to make some adjustments to the pressure switch on the fish intake hopper first."

And so Jacob fiddled about till midnight. There was no way that he was going to take the gamble of starting on a Friday, but no reference was ever made to the fact.

The new boat was a 'Viksund' 25ft fibre glass boat, powered by an 8hp single cylinder diesel engine. She was just what we needed, and named *Finnmark* after Norway's most northerly county. I would have preferred a 16hp twin cylinder, but Jacob had informed me that the bigger engine could not be delivered on time. He did some calculations, and found that the two cylinder engine would have got me across the harbour two minutes faster: "But what are you going to do with that extra two minutes?"

When the new machinery was set in motion, the difference was as daylight to dark. No more 'fish soup' would pour out onto the floor. The new cooking process was by indirect heated surfaces as opposed to live steam injection, which had been a headache for so many years. Steam was now available in abundance from the new oil fired boiler.

A vibrating screen replaced the de-watering screw conveyer. A new twin screwed press did a much more effective job.

The new Rotadisk drier was heated by steam. The new automatic fish oil separator would run for a whole week before being stripped down to be cleaned. A sea-water operated scrubber, helped to reduce the smell going to the atmosphere and last, but not least, the installation of a new three stage stick water (fish liquid) evaporator plant made a tremendous difference to efficiency and profitability. The meal yield rose from 16% to 20% equating to 4 tons extra meal produced from every 100 tons of fish processed. With the installation of new machinery, production rose from 9,267 tons in 1967 to 23,594 tons in 1968.

One evening, I had been testing fish oil in the lab and had poured the discarded sample with high ether content down the drain. I was doing some work in the office, adjacent to the lab when George Williamson came in. He was smoking a cigarette, and as he came past the sink, where I had just discarded the oil sample, shook the cigarette ash into it. There was a mighty explosion as flames shot to the ceiling. George would not use that ashtray again, and it would be the last time that I poured ether down a drain.

Harry S. Tulloch joined the workforce in April 1968. Harry reminds me that he was given little time to prepare for his new employment. He was ploughing on his croft when he received my relayed message at 4 o' clock in the afternoon, which was: "Can you be at Heogan at 6pm for a 12-hour nightshift?"

Harry became a great asset to the company. He started work as a plant operator then as boiler-man/shift engineer until promoted to foreman in 1975. In 1986 he was promoted to assistant manager, remaining in employment until HBP stopped trading in October 1990. He was employed by the new company as production manager from 1990 until he resigned in 1998.

Harry wisely took care of some company records, which would otherwise have been lost. He has kindly made these available as reference for this book. The records are not complete, but have been invaluable in compiling a list of employee names and times of their employment.

Maurice Anderson.

In mid summer 1968 Maurice Anderson, on leaving school, was employed full time in the office. He was a very pleasant and competent young man, taking care of the book work for ten years – prior to taking on the duties as assistant manager.

Many students found employment in the meal store at Heogan during their summer vacation. They came from far and wide. One student was to become the future Dr Jonathan Wills. Jonathan's short career in the meal store was in the early 1970s. He reminded me recently that he got a bad rash from the fish meal and, on returning home to Clodisdale, had to jump into the Setter Loch to clean up.

Jonathan Wills.

Angus Tulloch became a seaman at an early age, but in August 1966, he did work one 8-hour shift at Heogan. His reward was £2-04-00.

During his student days Jan Robert Riise, another Bressay man, spent his Easter breaks and summer vacations as painter and plant operator at Heogan. It was a great way of earning money to pay down his student loans, he says.

Alistair Christie-Henry spent his summer vacations in the meal store from 1968 to1973. One day I found him fast asleep on the meal stack. Alistair's main concern was that I would inform his father. "Please don't tell the old man," he said. "He will kill me." Alistair reminds me that the meal stores were full to capacity during a seaman's strike in 1968, and that we got extra storage space for meal at the Hoversta farm.

Jan Robert Riise.

Students from out-with the island stayed in caravans on the site. It was at the time of the magic mushrooms, which some of them either ate or smoked. The effects were quite dramatic. One early morning the shift foreman discovered one of them crawling around naked eating grass. The confused fellow believed that he had become a 'hedgehog'. Following that incident his by-name stuck.

Robert Bishop was more mature. He made his 'home' in a disused pump house near the water dam. His place of residence was duly dubbed 'The Cathedral'.

Charlie Stove was by no means a student. He had worked at the Heogan and also at the Aith Voe factory in the 1930s. Charlie was originally from Sandwick. He married my aunt, Annie Tulloch, and made his home on Bressay. With the revival at Heogan, Charlie expressed an interest to work one day in the meal store. For his 8-hours work he earned £4-08-00. It was on a Sunday. Charlie is on the Aith Voe photo from the 1930s as well an early photo at Heogan.

Roger Donald was one of the new employees in 1968. He was pleasant, reliable and capable, and became a great asset to the company. He worked firstly as an oil separator operator, and was later promoted to shift foreman, a position which he held until he retired in 1990. For some reason, Roger was accident prone, and if something adverse was about to happen, Roger would be there.

We had a safety committee, over which I presided. It worked very well; any suspect item brought to the attention of the committee was recorded, and given an item number. If a particular item had not been attended to by the next month's meeting, the outstanding item was transferred to the new list. In that way, things eventually got done. One day Roger asked me to accompany him to look at something which he said was a hazard. When I asked what it was, he pointed to a steel roof truss which crossed a catwalk.

"It's that beam," he said and as he turned round, smacked his head into it, obviously not for the first time. His priority was to keep the workplace clean and tidy and if it was raining, without fail Roger could be seen happily washing down the pier. At the end of the 1969 season Roger, Tommie Manson, Jamie Craigie and Magnie Tulloch, went to Norway to work for several weeks at Christian Bartz-Johannessen's factory on Sotra.

Jamie Cumming was born in Burra Isle in 1928; he had grown up with the sea and boats. In his working life Jamie had been a fisherman, gone to the Antarctic whaling, and later became a merchant seaman. He started work at Heogan in November 1968 as a crew member on MV *Shanty*.

Jamie Cumming.

He was a pleasant man, competent, reliable and trustworthy. Sadly, Jamie got a stroke in February 1975. When he recovered sufficiently from his illness, he was employed as cook in the canteen. In the late 1980s, as result of cut backs, he was made redundant.

During his fishing career, Jamie was a crew member on MV *Replenish*. This is the amazing story of events on board the 75ft *Replenish*, in January 1957, as told by him.

The *Replenish* left Burra Isle early on a Monday morning and had reached the fishing grounds north west of Shetland before daybreak. The weather had by then deteriorated, with an increasing north westerly wind and driving snow. Skipper John Pottinger saw that it was not fishing weather and set course back to Scalloway. Other boats in the area had already left.

Suddenly the *Replenish* breached as she was hit by a lump of water (a huge wave). Everything on deck was swept overboard by the impact, including the crew and galley where they were seated. Most of the wooden wheelhouse went over the side along with the radio and navigational equipment. The skipper caught hold of the rail as he was thrown by the sea and in sheer desperation was able to climb back onboard. The mate (John's son) was in his bunk below deck. He became trapped there by an upturned table and other objects that had been thrown about. The 17ft lifeboat, like everything else, had been swept overboard.

Amazingly Jamie, who could not swim, surfaced under the upturned lifeboat. He said that he had to dive in order to get free. The rest of the crew were struggling nearby and together they succeeded in righting the lifeboat and somehow managed to scramble on board.

The *Replenish* engine was still running and with her steering gear intact was making headway, but the net and ropes were hanging over the stern. John quickly disengaged the clutch to stop the propeller turning and, with the aid of his son, started to cut away the ropes. Then, to their amazement, they spotted the lifeboat and crew on the crest of a wave. With renewed vigour they fought to clear the debris from the stern.

What happened next is incredible. The *Replenish* and its lifeboat drifted together as if guided by the hand of God. All hands had miraculously been saved from the sea without human intervention.

John Pottinger was a very religious man and Jamie firmly believed that it was John's faith that saved their lives that day.

To the amazement of onlookers, the *Replenish* arrived under her own steam at Scalloway, minus a wheelhouse. With

Jamie Cumming fishing off the Bard.

the loss of their radio, John had not been able to raise the alarm.

That traumatic incident left its mark on Jamie, shattering his confidence somewhat, but he remained confident enough, even after a stroke, to fish and set creels from his Shetland model boat with its 1½hp Stuart Turner engine.

I tried in vain to persuade him to wear a lifejacket. In the end I said to his wife, Sheena: "Go to LHD and buy him one as a present," and amazingly, he wore it.

At Heogan, a tame crow was causing disruptions to the Tulloch family. If we left the door open, the crow would immediately come into the kitchen to steal something. He would invariably remove the pegs from our clothes line and Bjarnhild's washing ended up on the ground. One day in sheer frustration, I picked up the shotgun and shot it. In the process of doing so I tripped, twisting my ankle. Jamie was very serious as I limped in to the office: "Man you should never shoot a tame crow" he said.

Following that incident, it was like 'Murphy's Law' at Heogan, when for three weeks, everything that could go wrong, went wrong.

During that period 'The crow strikes again' became the slogan with the factory workers. The saga ended one night after we had gone to bed. I was asleep when the shift foreman tapped on our window, about two in the morning. "There's been an accident!" he shouted, bringing me instantly to life. "Chris Jacobson has lost his fingers."

It transpired that Chris, while attempting to clear a meal blockage had stuck his hand into a rotating valve.

Chris was brought in to our house; he had lost all four fingers on his right hand. His hand was submerged in flour to stop the bleeding, something that I learned at school from our navigation teacher, Captain Donnie Sinclair. Bjarnhild provided warm, sugary tea and rolled cigarettes for him. Chris was promptly taken to casualty at Gilbert Bain Hospital.

In 1968, the adoption papers finally came through for Bjarnhild's two sons and I officially became their father, something that I would never regret. The boys were very pleased with their new status and without prompting, immediately started to call me Dad. By then they had got a good grounding in English, starting with special tuition from Stella Sutherland. Stella was a good teacher and in the process of teaching the boys, she picked up a good smattering of Norwegian. She has retained an interest for their wellbeing until the present day.

The Replenish *at Scalloway.*   Robert Johnson

Herring drifters Responsive *LK37,* Enterprise *LK447,* Ocean Reaper *LK64, 1963.*
                                                              Robert Johnson

Ocean Reaper *LK64 in Scalloway Harbour. She was one of the last three drift net herring boats seen here in 1973. In the wheelhouse is George Hunter and on the stern are Robert Christie and Sammy Christie.* Robert Johnson

Gratitude *with 120 crans of herring arriving at Scalloway. Standing for'ard is Willie Halcrow and Walter Inkster, 1970.* Robert Johnson

The crew of the Replenish *LK97, the last drift net herring fishing crew in Shetland, 1975. From left: Sam Pottinger, Robert Christie, Lowrie Anderson, Stanley Pottinger, David Simmons, Walter Mouat, Ertie Pottinger, George W. Inkster, John Ridland. In the wheelhouse is skipper John William Pottinger.*   Robert Johnson

Fishing vessels blockade Lerwick harbour in a week of protest over cheap fish imports, 1975. In line from left – nearest to camera: Good Tidings, Replenish, Dauntless II *and* La Morlaye; *beyond them:* Concord, John West, Fortuna, Athena, Evening Star, Langdale, Compass Rose *and* Serene.   Robert Johnson

Serene, *July 1960, with 147 crans on board.*   *Robert Johnson*

10

The 1960s – Part five

SANDY LIPPE arrived from Fraserburgh to assemble a 250 ton capacity, rectangular fish oil tank. It was the time when things were coming to life at Heogan. Sandy was a blacksmith to trade, and soon had a forge and anvil going in the workshop. During his years at Heogan, he did some great work. If a conveyor chain broke, you could see Sandy quite happily sitting among the fish, and just like Heckie Macdonald in the 1950s, didn't turn a hair at getting dirty. Nevertheless, when Sandy did a job, no matter what it was, it was done to perfection.

I frequently discussed new ideas with Sandy, to get his opinion. He would either say: "That's a good idea," or if he thought that it had no merit, would say so, throwing in a few well-chosen adjectives to add weight.

Sandy stayed in a caravan during the week and went home to Scalloway at the weekend. There was only one problem, which was Monday mornings. The problem was solved by extending his weekend to include Mondays. Sandy never went back to Fraserburgh. He worked at Heogan until he retired in 1990.

My father in law, Bjarne Wian, came to stay with us in 1969. Bjarne was a native of the Lofoten Islands. As a young man he moved north to Kirkenes in order to find work at the iron ore company. Bjarne had remarkable endurance, working on maintenance of the company railway in extreme weather conditions for over forty years. In addition to his regular work, he became a volunteer fire fighter in Kirkenes during World War II. As the war escalated, fire fighting became a full time occupation. The years of stress, however, left its mark on him. Bjarne was 63 when he came to stay in Shetland and could not speak a word of English. Consequently, much Norwegian was spoken in our house at that time.

With Stella Sutherland's influence he began to understand the language a bit better. I became very fond of the old man and we learned much from each other. He loved Shetland, and when his health improved, he became a great asset to the family and kept the Norwegian language alive with his grandsons. Having grown up in the Lofoten Islands, he loved fishing and was an excellent cook, especially when it came to fish dishes. He spent his last 17 years here on Bressay.

Following the installation of new machinery in 1968, the factory became more dependent on landings from foreign vessels. By the early 1970s I could converse in Norwegian which was invaluable in communicating with Norwegian, Danish and Faroese fishermen. Danish industrial fishing boats had become a familiar sight as they lay sheltering at Lerwick waterfront, sometimes for a week or more while winter storms raged. I made a point of going on board the boats as soon as they arrived; to make it known that there was a factory at Heogan.

Communicating with the Danes was difficult at first, when I understood about a third of what was being said, but that improved with time. For a number of years, many Danes delivered their catches at Heogan. The smell of the fish they landed was often appalling. It was so bad in the factory house that sometimes we had to move out. Bjarnhild was convinced that her clothes must have smelt of the factory when she went to Lerwick.

There was, however, one bonus from the Danish boats. They often had a few good halibut on board, resulting in many great meals for us. One day a Faroese boat arrived at the pier with no fish onboard. The skipper had come to ask a favour. He wanted to borrow a pump. I said that there was no problem in borrowing the pump but that there was a cost involved. "How much will it cost?" he asked.

A prime halibut was hanging up between decks and I pointed towards it: "That one."

He smiled and confirmed that it was a deal. Knowing the Faroese tendency to hang fish and meat to 'ripen', I enquired how long it had hung there.

"Oh that one is just right. We were about to cut it up to put in the deep freeze."

It was much easier to cut them up after the skin had dried for a few hours he explained. The barter, however, included a dinner of Shetland lamb for the Faroese crew.

A phone call to the manager of the fish meal and oil factory at Fuglafjord in Faroe, led to regular contact between the two factories.

Thereafter, when their factory got congested, the manager arranged for their boats to deliver at Heogan. Many came back on a regular basis.

Icelandic boats also landed their catches at Heogan. Two boats fished on contract to the factory for many weeks. The first to deliver was *Thordur Jonasson*; the skipper was Simon Thordurson. His first delivery to Heogan was an amazing sight, with sillocks swimming in two feet of water on the deck. I have never before or after, seen a boat so overloaded. They landed 330 tons of herring that day, a record landing at the time. Simon was a pleasant fellow and became a regular visitor to our house. He was over six and a half feet tall and to avoid hitting his head, had developed the habit of bending down each time he came through a door.

Simon's purse net, at 110 metres deep, was designed for the deep water around Iceland. In the shallower waters around Shetland his net got snagged in the bottom. Following each landing, the crew spent two days repairing the huge net on the Freshers pier.

Simon's wife was Norwegian. He told us that she got very homesick living in Iceland. Each time she went back to Norway, Simon had to make a special trip with his boat to fetch her back.

The other Icelandic boat on contract was *Ethlady*, but I have forgotten the skipper's name. He was perhaps smarter than Simon. By reducing the depth of his net, he avoided constant repairs. Consequently, with a smaller boat, he landed more herring.

Another overloaded fishing boat comes to mind. The small Norwegian boat, *Nyegg*, with a three man crew arrived at Heogan unannounced. The skipper asked permission to land his catch of pout. As the pits were full to the brim I said that, unfortunately, we were unable to take delivery. The skipper looked extremely worried and agitated. If he went back to sea he said, they would never reach Norway. I could see that he was genuine and relented, providing that he was prepared to wait. Unbelievably, after discharging at Heogan, they went back to sea, overloading the boat once more. On their way back to Norway the boat sank with the loss of all hands.

It was impossible to accommodate everyone. There was an amusing episode when a persistent Norwegian skipper was refused permission to land. He talked to Bjarnhild asking her if she could persuade me to take his fish. After all, he had been shipmates with her brother! That argument didn't help him either.

11

THE 1970S – PART ONE

IN THE mid-1960s the Norwegian fleet combined with Icelandic, Faroese and Danes were exploiting herring stocks to the verge of extinction. The Norwegian fleet numbered some 250 boats fishing in waters around Shetland.

By 1970 there was much change within the Shetland fishing fleet. A new generation of fishing boats was replacing the drift netters.

The first purse seine vessel to join the fleet was the 92ft *Adalla*, bought second-hand from Norway by Dr Alistair Goodlad in 1967. Four new purse seine boats joined the fleet in 1969. They were *Wave Crest*, *Serene*, *Unity* and *Azalea*. Their landings at Heogan that year totalled 1,885 tons.

Mackie Polson had seen that the only way forward was to follow the path of the Norwegians. He and partners Willie Anderson, Dodie Polson, Robbie John Anderson and Gibbie Williamson got their new steel boat *Serene* built in Flekkefjord, Norway. Mackie engaged Paul Reite, (a young Norwegian who had obtained his skippers ticket) to show them the new technique in fishing. Mackie reminds me that in 1970 the new *Serene* made three full loads of herring at Heogan within 24 hours.

Without doubt, Mackie Polson was the fishing skipper that I got to know best. If I was not on the Heogan pier when he came along side, he would immediately appear in the office. No other fishing skipper did that. He had a great interest in the factory and was very much aware of its importance to the fishing community. I have looked on him as a friend for many years, but as tends to happen, we don't meet very often.

Mackie was born in Whalsay in 1928. His involvement in fishing started at an early age, collecting mussels and baiting haddock lines before and

Shetland's first purse seiners. From right: Azalea, Wavecrest, Serene *and* Unity *discharge their catches into boxes on Alexandra Wharf, Lerwick.*   *Martin Smith*

after school. One day, as he was wheeling a barrow laden with fishing lines towards Symbister, he met insurance agent Jamie Aitkin. Jamie was intrigued by the industrious young fellow, who did not really have time to go to school. Two weeks later Mackie, at the age of 13, was granted exemption from school.

Mackie's fishing career started in 1945 as cook and coiler on board the *Jeannie*. His fathers boat *Research* had been requisitioned by the war commission and following her release in 1946, Mackie became a crew member with his father- Bobby Polson. In the winter of 1946 Mackie did a season at the Antarctic whaling on board Salvesens factory ship *Southern Venturer*. In 1947, he was back on the *Research* prior to joining the *Betty Leslie* as driver. *Betty Leslie* did not have a reverse gear, the procedure was to stop the engine and then start it running in the opposite direction. Mackie went from mate to skipper on the *Betty Leslie.*

In 1955 Mackie with partners Willie Anderson and George (Dodie) Polson bought a new boat from Summer's yard in Fraserburgh at the cost of £14,000; she was named *Serene* LK 63. In time seven boats would bear the name *Serene*. Mackie retired from active fishing in 1990, when his son Bobby took over as skipper. Today, at the age of 84, Mackie is still alert and on the ball, retaining an interest in the family business. He still goes fishing each summer and has not missed a year at the herring fishing since his career began. The latest luxury class *Serene* was built in 2009 at the cost of £16,000.000.

As a rule, Bjarnhild and I travel to Aberdeen by sea, but once in the 1990s we travelled by air. Mackie and Janet were on the same flight and he said that they were going on to London. What he didn't tell me was that he was going to Buckingham Palace to be honoured by the Queen.

Mackie Polson at home in 2013, with his models of the first and current Serene.

When we met again some time later I remarked: "You might have told me why you were going to London, Mackie."

"It was the biggest embarrassment that ever came to Whalsay," said Mackie.

With ever increasing developments at Heogan, we were gradually getting hemmed in and knew that we would have to move house. Five years of living at the work place had been enough. The company offered to build a manager's house on a site of our choice, but we were not happy at the prospect of another tied house. Fortunately, Christian came to the rescue. "I think it is much better that we help him build his own house".

I contacted John Scott who was willing to sell us a house site at Cruester. In July 1970 I travelled to Norway and with the help of my friend, Jacob Bø, found an attractive house plan and signed a contract for the delivery of a timber house. While we were still at the planning stage, I met Willie Laurenson from Hillside, Heogan. He had heard that I was planning to build a new house. I confirmed that we had got a site at Cruester. "Too far away," was Willies remark, shaking his head.

When asked what he meant, he said that I would not be able to see the factory. "That is exactly why I am going over the hill, Willie. I don't want to see the factory."

The installation of new machinery in 1968 had been a step in the right direction. Production increased from 17,134 tons in 1969 to 29,635 tons in 1970, but the factory's capacity was still too low. It was decided to increase capacity in time for the 1971 season. During the early months of 1971 the old factory received more rough treatment, as a gang of Norwegians installed a second line of machinery. As in 1968, the ship lay

Aerial view of the Heogan factory, 1971.   *Bartz-Johannessen*

at anchor while the heavy lifts were landed by raft. The ship then berthed at Freshers pier to land the lightweight items.

Included in the cargo was our house kit. It was rather amusing to see our kitchen sink being swung ashore by a ten ton crane. To the amazement of the locals; two Norwegian joiners assembled the house kit on a concrete block basement in three and a half weeks. Ours was the first of a new generation of timber houses in Shetland and created a lot of interest.

Shetland economy took an upturn about that time. While our house was being erected, we had two visits from SIC Councillors to observe how the house was built. They asked many questions and were favourably impressed. Later that year, the council placed an order with Fjogstad in

Norway for delivery of 100 houses to accommodate essential incoming workers. The houses were erected at different locations throughout Shetland.

On 15th January 1972, we were delighted to move over the hill to our new home, one year to the day since the excavations began.

With the installation of a second line of new machinery in 1971, fish intakes increased to 36,215 tons, of which 62% were delivered by the local fleet. Shetlands drift net fleet suffered badly through the exploitation of herring stocks in the 1960s. In 1971 the local herring season started with 22 drifters of which only three were Shetland boats. Their catches were low and by the end of July only five remained. Their total landings totalled only 10,198 crans that season, compared to 66,787 by the purse seiners. A total of 13,610 tons herring was landed at Heogan by the local fleet that year. Drift net fishing in Shetland came to an end in 1975 when the Burra boat *Replenish* gave up after only a few weeks.

On 1st January 1977, a ban was imposed on herring fishing in parts of the North Sea. It marked the end of herring curing in Shetland. The

Bressay Up Helly Aa ex-Jarls, 1972. From left – back: James L. Matches, Hebbie Tulloch, George Williamson, Roger Donald, Graham Henderson, Tammie H. Manson. Front: Lol Anderson, Jim MacKay, Harry Tulloch, Charlie Christie-Henry, Jim Hardy.   *Dennis Coutts*

backbone of Shetlands economy for over 130 years had been broken by modern technology in the span of only 12 years.

Shetlands new purse seiners were also hit hard by the ban and were forced to turn their attention to the Minch fishery. When the Minch fishery was also closed in 1978, the Shetland boats joined Scottish boats in the lucrative mackerel fishery at Falmouth.

The gradual development at Heogan continued as additional pits were built, increasing the storage capacity to 1,200 tons. A roof was constructed over the pits to give shelter from the elements, and keep the seagulls at bay.

Thousands of tons of concrete were poured into foundations and roads. Jamie Henry and his gang were kept busy and the workforce peaked at fifty men.

Work on a new concrete road had just been completed, when we found that additional meal storage was required. I could see only one solution. We had to reclaim an area from the sea. There was one problem, however. Jamie's new road would have to go. I thought about it for a couple of days before broaching the subject. "Jamie, what would you say if I told you that your fine new road will have to be torn up?"

"What did you have in mind?" he asked.

When I showed him the layout plan, he said: "That's a damned good idea."

Tootsie Gray was contracted with his huge Leibherr excavator, and soon the fine new road, along with thousands of tonnes of rock, was infill for the new meal store. A replacement concrete road was built on a lower level, followed by a retaining sea wall. The foundations and floor were of course built by the gang. The next step was to erect a small silo, adjacent to the meal store. Thereafter, with more flexibility, the meal was all bagged on dayshift.

1973 was the year when a much needed canteen was built for the workers. The chosen site required much preparation, but the end result was worth the effort. It created a pleasant environment for the workers, with a fine view of the north harbour.

Harry Hunter was contracted to do the excavations, and the soil from our former garden was transported to our house site at Cruester. Harry later commented that it was the first time he had seen someone move house, and take their garden with them.

The canteen foundations were duly built by the construction gang. This was Jamie Henry's last project at Heogan. He decided it was time to move on, and opted for a less stressful job as storeman at P&O Ferries Ltd, where he worked until he retired.

The new canteen was purchased from Norway. The timber clad building was built to a high standard by Norwegian joiner Ottar Gjerdevik, and his assistant, Tom Hausvik. Complete with changing room, lockers and showers, it was a much needed facility for the workers.

A ruling was made that no dirty clothes or boots were allowed in the new canteen. This ruling was strictly adhered to, and resulted in facilities that everyone could be proud of.

Thirty-six years on, in May 2009, we got a pleasant surprise when Ottar, accompanied by his three daughters, dropped in. He had talked so much about Shetland over the years that his daughters arranged the trip to mark his seventieth birthday. It was great to meet Ottar again after all these years. He and Tom had lodged with us while building the canteen. There was much to talk about, and he took great pleasure in showing his daughters the canteen still standing there, as good as the day it was built.

As the size of fishing boats increased, shallow water at the factory pier restricted landings. It was decided to add a concrete extension to the wooden pier to give six metres depth of water at low tide. Provision for a fixed crane was included in the design. A Norwegian company was contracted to build the extension. The Norwegian team were namely: Magnus Aasheim, Hans Knapskog, Gunnar Hetland, Hans Storebø, Magnar Sivertsen, Birger Hauge and Frank Hauge. With help from our workforce, the job was done during May 1974.

Fish intake facilities were temporarily moved to the Freshers pier, requiring

Canteen staff Johnnie Clark, Hilda Black and Jon Noble from Fraserburgh..   Jean Anderson

Canteen staff Jimmy Cummings, Jean Anderson with Percy Aggutor.
Jean Anderson

Bert Henderson who worked for some years in the canteen..
Elizabeth Scollay

three tractors and trailers to transport the fish. On completion of the pier extension, a new fibre glass conveyor, with lids to keep the seagulls at bay, replaced the thirty year old wooden conveyor.

On the day that the new pier facilities were put into service, the Fraserburgh registered boat, MV *Taits,* arrived with a full load of horse mackerel. While they were discharging, the Whalsay boat *Serene,* came along side to land a few baskets of herring. As skipper Mackie Polson was in a hurry to get back to sea, one of the lids was removed in order to gain access to the conveyor.

Few things in my life have affected me like what happened next. I was in the office when someone came running in to inform me that a man had been killed on the pier and advised that I should call the police. Instead, I ran down to the pier to find out first hand what had happened. By the time I arrived at the pier, the *Taits* had left and were heading for Lerwick at full speed.

Lollie Sutherland was pier man that day. From him, I learned what had happened. It transpired that Andrew Tait, a retired fishing skipper, and then an elderly man, had accompanied his sons on the fishing trip. Out of curiosity, Andrew climbed up a ladder to look into the hopper above the hectolitre measure. Lollie saw the man there, and instructed him to come down immediately. Andrew turned round, lost his balance, and fell into the moving conveyor.

Lollie took immediate action, running as fast as he could to the nearest emergency stop button. It immerged that a conveyor lid had been left

off. Unbelievably, when the conveyor came to a halt, there was Andrew lying among the fish, right under the second opening. Had the conveyor stopped at any other point it could have taken some time to find him as there were many nuts and bolts securing the lids.

When Andrew was found, his two sons used a ladder as a makeshift stretcher. An ambulance met the boat, taking him to the Gilbert Bain Hospital where he was diagnosed as having a few broken bones, but miraculously, he survived.

Needless to say, an additional stop button was installed near the place of the accident. Thankfully, it was never needed. The old wooden conveyor had run for more than 30 years, without an emergency stop button in place.

Lollie Sutherland at 80.

96

A favourite pastime for some individuals was to sketch portraits of their workmates. Some of the work was very good but it was getting a bit out of hand. Pots of paint were therefore issued with instructions to clean up the place. Alex Priest, originally from Elgin, was the pit man. His job entailed operating a hydraulic digger which assisted feeding a screw conveyor in the sloping bottom. The pit man was required to wear safety harness, clipped onto an overhead wire, running lengthwise above the pits division wall.

When the assistance of the digger was not required, the pit man spent his time in a small lookout hut. The hut had become a favourite artist's studio. Alex's commented regarding the clean up was: "There was wan there o' me that I did'na like to paint oot. They had got wings on me."

I have written about Bressay men working in Orkney during the 1950s. The role was reversed, when more prosperous times reached Shetland. One Orcadian to find work at Heogan was Jamie Craigie. He came to Bressay as a lighthouse keeper. When notified of a shift of station, Jamie opted to retire from the lighthouse service, and sought work at Heogan. He was very reliable, working as separator operator until 1975 when, with several others, he got work at Norscot. Jamie was a good fiddle player and played with the local band at functions in the Bressay Hall.

Arthur Wylie was another Orcadian who worked at Heogan. He sold his farm in Orkney and moved to Bressay, following his marriage to a local girl.

In spite of being a bit slow in the uptake, Arthur was a good worker. He was a kind person, and was very popular with his workmates at Heogan. Bertie Birnie in particular made an effort to show Arthur easier ways of doing things. Arthur was easy to please. The company provided protective clothing for the workers, and Arthur needed new boots. When asked what size he wore, he held up his foot. "Well they're no that big" he said. Checking the records, we found that his previous issues had ranged in sizes from 7 to 11.

When Arthur retired in 1984 after seven years service in the company, his workmates laid on a party in the canteen for him. Sadly his retirement was to be all too short.

Another Orcadian who was employed indirectly at Heogan was Wilfie Bruce. He worked as an apprentice joiner with building contractors, T. L. Arcus. I remember Wilfie as a young man, replacing skylights on the cement asbestos clad factory roof. Many years later, when we met on a salmon farm, Wilfie said: "I remember the first words you said to me."

"Oh, what was that Wilfie?"

"You tapped me on the shoulder and said, 'Walk on the beams, it's a long way down."

Perhaps I was thinking about a man at the Fraserburgh factory, who fell forty feet, when the brittle sheeting gave way. Luckily that man escaped serious injury, as he glanced off a metal cyclone on the way down to cushion his fall.

12

THE 1970S – PART TWO

AS A BOY, Dag had an interest in anything mechanical or electrical. While still at school, he bought a kit and built an oscilloscope.

The old radio with a short wave band, which I had used to tune in to the drift net herring fleet in the 1950s, had long since stopped working. It stood on a shelf in the office gathering dust. I took it to a radio repair shop in Lerwick, asking for an assessment. Dag came with me to collect the radio. The verdict was: 'Beyond economical repair'.

On the way back to Heogan I picked up the old radio: "Why am I taking this old thing home, if it cannot work?" and was just about to throw it over the side, when Dag cut in quickly: "If you're going to dump it, can I have it?" As soon as we got home, he opened it up, gave it a thorough going over with a vacuum cleaner and switched it on and surprisingly, it worked.

Dag repeated his last year at Anderson high school in order to pass higher grade exams. On leaving school he started a four years electrical apprenticeship with J.F.M. in Lerwick. A holiday in Norway, however, led to a change of direction for him. He decided that he wanted to move back to Norway. Breaking the news to me he added that I needn't argue.

I hadn't even started arguing and furthermore, had no intention of doing so. It is everyone's right to choose what they want to do in life. With the assurance that no argument was forthcoming, Dag relaxed: "But I don't want to go yet. I want to go to a Technical School in Norway and need to save some money first. Will you give me a job here at the factory for one year?"

Having already done a stint in the meal store, during his summer holidays, he knew the score. In the following year, he worked every available hour and saved £1200, which was quite a sum of money at the time.

In 1975, Dag enrolled at the Technical school at Rubbestadneset on the island of Bømlo, Norway. After a year there, he got work at Wichman Motor Fabrikk, working on remote control systems. Incidentally, that is the factory where the traditional single cylinder engines for fishing boats were made. During World War II, essential spare parts for the Shetland Bus boats were secretly made there, to be smuggled to Shetland under the noses of the enemy. The company is now under new ownership, but 36 years on, Dag, with several changes of direction, is still working there. He married Irene, a local girl, who also works at the same factory, as do their two sons. Dag is now the proud grandfather of three.

Rune was a happy boy, creating many hilarious situations by his antics. One day he went hunting with bow and arrow, the seagulls were his targets; they were in such abundance that it would be difficult to miss. Rune crept under the elevator to take aim, but in doing so he tripped and fell into the sea. He was rescued from his perch on a tide stringer by Ray Tulloch; his future father in law.

That day, Rune got his first glass of whisky before a hot bath and being put to bed. He did not utter one word until the following morning. Another day, Rune rushed in very excitedly to inform his mother that he had seen a huge fish, swimming near the pier.

"What kind of fish was it" Bjarnhild asked?

"I'm not sure" he said, "But I think it was either a cod or a lutefisk."

Lutefisk is a Norwegian speciality, where dried fish are submerged in a caustic soda solution and then watered out to get rid of the caustic. It takes eight days to make the dinner.

Then there was the morning following an autumn gale when our vegetable garden was destroyed by wind and salt spray. Rune had left for school but returned very seriously to inform his mother that the whole garden had gone rusty.

With so much influence of the factory around him, it came as no surprise that he showed interest of making a career at Heogan. In 1973, he started a four-year apprenticeship in mechanical engineering with block release courses at Inverness Technical College. Christian Bartz-Johannessen was very pleased to hear the news and told me that he hoped Rune would one day follow in my footsteps as manager.

Rune worked under the supervision of Sandy Lippe, getting a good general grounding. Among other things, he became a very good welder. After nine years at Heogan, Rune changed direction to become self-employed. He also worked as a mechanic at the Sullom Voe Oil Terminal for some time, before returning to Heogan as engineering manager in 1990.

He worked in that capacity until 1996. The photos of the transporting and erecting of the new factory in 1982, were taken by Rune.

Rune and Fiona moved to Aberdeenshire in 1999 with their family of four. They are now blessed with three lively grandchildren. He is currently working for a local farm produce company, where he has responsibility for maintenance of machines in their food processing factory. Rune's interest in sports led him to coach ice-hockey for 10 years. Among the young players was his son Philip, who has become a very good ice-hockey player.

Robin Strachan, like many fellow Shetlanders, served on Salvesen's whaling factory ships in the south Atlantic. He held a key job as operator of the Bovril plant. When commercial whale-catching stopped about 1960, Robin was one of the few employees to be retained by the company. He and a Norwegian friend got an offer of work at fish reduction plants in Peru.

Robin was very versatile and had an ear for languages. His knowledge of evaporation plants, coupled with his ability to converse in both Norwegian and Spanish, led to his promotion with overall responsibility for the company's numerous evaporation plants.

Robin met and married a Peruvian girl and lived there for several years where their eldest two daughters were born. In June 1973 he returned to his native Bressay with his wife and family. Due to fog, the regular air service was cancelled, but that did not stop Robin getting home. Accompanied by his family he arrived in Shetland by helicopter.

With his knowledge of evaporation plants, Robin was the obvious choice as a plant operator at Heogan. He worked there until 1975 when he got alternative employment at an oil service supply base in Lerwick.

In 1974 while at a conference in Denmark I met one of Robin's Norwegian friends from his former days. On hearing that I was from Bressay, the man asked: "Do you know Robin Strachan?"

"Yes I know him very well. He is a relative of mine. He is now working as evaporator man at our factory."

"Robin was a great guy; does he still like a dram?"

Confirming that Robin had always liked a dram, a smile broke on the man's face: "I will tell you a little story from our early days in Peru. One night when Robin had just one too many, he fell asleep in his car. Some of the local boys came past and while Robin was sleeping, lifted the car onto wooden blocks and removed all four wheels."

Back at Heogan, I was doing my usual rounds, and stopped to talk to Robin. When the subject turned to Peru I asked: "How were the natives to work with?"

"Oh they were lovely people" he said, "but they were terrible for stealing."

"Yes, I believe that they would even steal the wheels of your car if you didn't keep your wits about you."

Robin gave me a strange look, but I never enlightened him that I had met his friend.

With the arrival in 1975, of M.V. *Grima*, Bressay's first car ferry, life on the island changed forever. It was now possible to drive to Lerwick, and even to take a car onboard P&O Ferries to Aberdeen. Life had suddenly become so much simpler, but there was also a downside.

People now sat in their cars being ferried to Lerwick, as opposed to congregating on board the *Brenda* where women and children sat in the cabin and the men stood out in the open aft. A weekly trip to Lerwick with the *Brenda* had also been a social occasion where people talked and exchanged news.

Many islanders were related in some way and the community resembled a large family. Bressay has always had a turnover in population, with people leaving the island while others moved in. It had been a gradual process and in the past, newcomers quickly fitted into the community. With the new ferry service, the process accelerated and for the first time I no longer knew everyone on the island.

The positive side of change quickly outweighed the negative, however, and there cannot be many who would willingly turn the clock back. The advantages of the car ferry were great for the factory. Transport to and from Lerwick was now done by cars, vans or trucks, and *Shanty*, which had served so well for nine years, became redundant. An added advantage was that heavy plant and machinery could now be transported on the ferry.

Earlier attempts to buy land for development had failed, due to a dispute with the land owner, Willie Jacobson. In 1978 the situation changed when Eric Fillmore bought the land surrounding the factory. Eric was a kind man and did not drive a hard bargain. On request he immediately sold the desired area to HBP and plans were made to build a new factory. The site was partially excavated, but a 48% drop in production that year resulted in the development being shelved.

Eric, who had an engineering background from his service in the Royal Navy, was employed as boiler man /mechanic. He was very thorough in his work, but one day Eric's attempt at perfection backfired. One of the boilers cut out while the factory was working to full capacity. The problem was simply a build-up of carbon in the burner. To remove the carbon was about fifteen minutes work. I was not amused to discover why it was taking so long to get the boiler back on line – Eric had decided to strip down the entire assembly and give it a coat of paint.

Electrics have never been my strongpoint and I have always relied on the services of a qualified electrician in that direction. Prior to 1964, the electrical installation at Heogan was fairly basic. The Lerwick based firm, S.E.P.S. did maintenance on a regular basis.

In the mid-1960s Magnie Ratter became our first full-time electrician. He was a likable fellow and full of fun. He and Beth stayed on Bressay for some years, where their two children were born. The electrical installation at the factory like everything else was showing its age, resulting in frequent breakdowns.

When a fault developed, Magnie would soon find it and in the space of a few minutes, string out a temporary lead to get the motor back on line. As time went on the temporary leads became quite numerous. During a lull in production, however, he eventually got things tidied up and back to normal.

Colin Henry was our next full-time electrician, followed by Andrew Paton. They were both first class electricians, especially regarding new installations. Peter Smith also served as shift electrician for some time.

One day, production was brought to a standstill. Andrew was puzzled; a series of checks showed that everything electrical was functional. Eventually he found the problem however. It was simply a matchstick which had got lodged in a solenoid valve.

Robbie Eunson was born in 1908 at Traewick, a remote township on the east side of Whalsay. His family moved to Bressay about 1920 where his father took tenancy of a croft at Grindischool and built a new house there.

During World War II, Robbie and Jamie Deyell from Bressay were shipmates onboard the Merchant Navy ship *Clan Ferguson*. Their ship, which was part of a Malta convoy during 1942, was torpedoed and sunk. A full account of their ordeal as

Peter Smith, Lerwick. Daisy Smith

prisoners of war, written by Barbara Anderson, can be seen at Bressay Heritage Centre. A great deal of work has gone into her research. Most of her information came from Jamie's small secret diary which he wrote during their years of captivity. Jamie described the horrendous treatment of prisoners during their estimated 725 mile forced march from the centre of Poland to Hildesheim in West Germany. It is quite evident that without Jamie's unfailing help and attention, Robbie could not have survived.

Robbie, like his father, was good with his hands. After the war he worked as a local handyman on Bressay and was never idle. While cutting peat in 1956, I was intrigued to see his portable cooker in use. It was made from an old bucket with a hand driven, forced-draught fan attached. He had made a replica of what they used during their forced march through Europe.

Robbie taught woodwork through the further education scheme for a time. One day, an elderly woman asked if he would take a look at her saw: "What's wrong with your saw, Anna?" he asked.

"Well when I use him, I dinna get ony sawdust," she said.

When things started to come to life at Heogan I was delighted to able to employ Robbie as part of the construction gang.

Jamie worked as road foreman on Bressay for some years. He also became part of the Heogan construction gang for a time. In 1975 he went back to work for the SIC, constructing a breakwater in preparation for the arrival of Bressay's first car ferry.

Among his many talents, Robbie was a bit of a poet. George Birnie kindly gave me a copy of this poem, where Robbie gives his version of working at Heogan. BOGO was the company which owned the factory until 1935. Many of the older generation, my father included, referred to the factory as 'Da Bogo'.

Wirkin at Da Bogo

Dir getting a new factory up in Yell
But we hae an auld aen, tae wirsell
Though the Lerock folk canno stand da smell
 It's a gold mine at da Bogo

Some men wirk, an count dir gains
An some goes aff, wi aches an pains
While som just come tae dig oot Danes
 Fishing for da Bogo

Dey wir Itallians an Frogies
Dey wir Poles an dey wir Yogies
An aye dey wid hae dir peerie soggies
     Diggin at da Bogo

We hae a blue Shanty *fur da auld gut run*
An'in stormy wadder da crew tinks it's fun
Dey ken dir nae danger wi a boddam lik yon
     Dir sure tae mak da Bogo

Inside da lower door amidst din an' clatter
You'll see a poor chap among stick water
I doot if he ever gets ony fatter
     Wirkin for da Bogo

Nixt you come tae da separater
An' dere you'll see anider poor crater
Some times you'd need a good inflater
     Wirkin for da Bogo

Nixt you come tae da press an' drier
Dis new ane doisno' need a fire
Just turn on whit steam you require
     Wirkin at da Bogo

If you look next door you'll see Magnie at it
Da boiler dey say is automatic
But sometimes it's a bit eratic
     Wirkin at da Bogo

When he needs water he rings a bell
Dan Robbie comes doon an' plays up hell
Thirty thousand gallons oot o' da Coonty well
     A' gone tae da Bogo

If you go oot da back door you'll see da pit
Lipperin tae da brim wi shit
An der you'll see a poor man sit
     Wirkin for da Bogo

Dan if you go oot an turn left wheel
You'll come tae da place whare dey bag da meal
An whin you look inside it makes you feel
    Its grim wark at da Bogo

Wan fellow got exempt fur a rashy reason
Annider ane cudno stop fae sneezing
While a third man nearly lost his reason
    Wirkin at da Bogo

Heed jump aboot an' screech an snoar
Dan at Jeamie he gaed a roar
But Jeamie threw him oot da door
    Wirkin at da Bogo

Noo boys I tink yon ends me tell
I'm meby no teld it awful well
But as I sit here I can still smell
    Da perfume fae da Bogo

Robbie Eunson.   Andy Dalziel

Ian Hughes was born in Scalloway, son of George Hughes a herring curer in Shetland. Following his education at Lerwick central school, Ian served an apprentiship as a cooper in his father's business. Later he did business studies and gained employment at a higher level in the salt herring trade. Apart from his war service, Ian worked in the herring industry throughout his working life. He worked for Smith and Shultz of Peterhead and in the Western Isles and later with Associated Herring Merchants, in conjunction with Leslie & Company in Aberdeen. Leslie & Co. had been involved with HBP from the outset.

The two companies shared offices in the same building in Aberdeen, firstly at 32 Schoolhill, and finally at 8-10 Victoria Street. With the ever changing scene, Ian got directly involved with HBP. He became a company director in 1963. When George Reid was preparing for retirement, Ian became more involved with the factories and became managing director in 1981.

With Ian at the wheel, I was given almost a free hand to do things as I saw fit. Regarding technical matters, I had direct contact with the Bergen office, especially with engineer Jacob Bø who had become a good friend.

Ian served with The Gordon Highlanders during the war. In 1944 he was seriously wounded in his back, head and left arm, and as a result spent a whole year in a Glasgow hospital. Ian was left handed, but in spite of his injuries, was able to go back to work when the herring industry came on stream again in 1946. He was very good at figures and could count three columns of figures simultaneously, without the use of a calculator. Ian married Eleanor in September 1946. He is survived by a son who lives in Aberdeen and a daughter in Jamaica. Eleanor and I still correspond at Christmas.

13

THE 1980S – PART ONE

MANY different species have been processed at Heogan over the years, with fluctuation in landings between local and foreign vessels. Prior to the sand eel fishery of the 1980s, part of the Shetland fleet followed in the footsteps of Danes, Faroese and Norwegians to fish for industrial species. Pout fishing commenced on a local level in 1968, when landings at Heogan totalled 77 tons, as opposed to the 9,491 tons landed by foreign boats. Local pout fishery reached a peak in 1974 with 18,219 tons, as opposed to 2,473 tons delivered by foreign vessels.

The sand eel fishery which started in 1974 and continued into the 1990s was of great importance to the factory; it was the main species to be processed at Heogan at that time. Sand eel make excellent fish meal and have moderate oil content. It gives a good yield, provided that it is processed within 36 hours of being caught; beyond that time, enzymes break down the fish. Despite a relatively good throughput in 1979, the company balance sheet showed a loss at Heogan. This was why we were losing money; a large percentage was simply disappearing down the drain.

At the start of the 1980 season, I called all the workers to a meeting, informing them that we had lost money in 1979 and explained why. As I saw it, 1980 would be a make or break year for the factory. Something had to change. It was imperative to process the eels within 36 hours of being caught. How could it be done when the boats came in with full catches on a Friday? The answer was simple. Instead of stopping production on Saturday, as was normal practice, I proposed to work through the weekend, then have a midweek break to clean the machines and change shift rotation. The workers agreed without exception, and the new arrangement paid off.

At a fishermen's meeting in April 1980 I reported what had been decided at Heogan. An agreement was reached to set a weekly quota. The new agreement worked well for all concerned. 22,283 tons of eels were landed by the local fleet that summer. The local fishery peaked in 1981 when 36,016 tons were landed.

From April until mid-September 1982, 35.000 tons of sand eels were processed with good results. Thirty two boats and 166 men fished for the factory, giving the local economy a boost of £1 million. Despite the fact that the greater part of the fleet was fishing for industrial species, 211 tons of gutted white fish ended up as mink food that year. It was evident that Shetland's fishing industry would have been in a poorer state without an outlet at Heogan.

Many Shetland boats fished sand eels exclusively for the factory during the summer months from 1974 till 1995. As their contribution was so great for the survival of the factory, the following list has been compiled. It is for the season of 1983, where detailed records have been found. Here are details of landings made by the 26 Shetland boats.

Ardsheean. *Martin Smith*

Aquilla. *Martin Smith*

Adenia	24 trips	2,155 tons
Andromeda	26 trips	869 tons
Aquilla	29 trips	2,066 tons
Avrella	37 trips	1,279 tons
Dewy Rose	54 trips	922 tons
Donvale	6 trips	238 tons
Franchise	73 trips	1,475 tons
Freedom	72 trips	1,022 tons
Good Tidings	28 trips	1,229 tons
Harvest Gold	67 trips	1,318 tons
Hercules	9 trips	179 tons
Horizon	32 trips	1,195 tons
Jessie Sinclair	38 trips	1,587 tons
Launch Out	22 trips	157 tons
Lustre	7 trips	41 tons
North Star	3 trips	59 tons
Opportune	29 trips	1.211 tons
Planet	14 trips	1,230 tons
Radiant Star	16 trips	677 tons
Snowdrop	67 trips	842 tons
Steadfast	50 trips	1,321 tons
Summer Rose	39 trips	497 tons
Sunbeam	28 trips	2,009 tons
Sunrise	42 trips	1,802 tons
Victory	2 trips	35 tons
Welfare	21 trips	915 tons

Donvale. *Martin Smith*

Krisona. *Martin Smith*

Three sand eel boats.. *Martin Smith*

Day Dawn. *Martin Smith*

Together they made 835 landings, amounting to 26,330 tons

Boats which were part of the fishery in 1982 and 1984 but not in 1983 were:

Fortuna	Starina
Starlight	Madalia
Unity	Morning Star
Araine	Nil Desperandum
Day Dawn	Osprey
Golden Gleam	Our Catherine
Flourish	Sonia
Julie Anne	

Starina *and* Ardsheean.
Martin Smith

Later in the decade larger boats from the north east coast regularly delivered big landings of sand eel at Heogan such as *Silvery Sea* with individual landings of 462 tons, *Baltasound* with 520 tons, *Jasper Sea* with 628 tons, *Chris Andra* with 338 tons and *Kross Fjord* with 302 tons.

For many years it had been the company's policy to pay the workers a Christmas bonus. The bonus at that time amounted to $100 per man.

In November 1980 a letter arrived from head office informing that no bonus would be paid at Christmas. I was not prepared to accept their decision, but neither a plea on the phone nor a letter to the directors bore fruit. My next step was to book a flight to Aberdeen. The company's argument was that they could not pay a bonus to the Bressay workers, and not to all other company employees. My argument was for the Bressay workers alone and that there was a principle at stake.

At the start of the season I had asked the men for their co-operation, and got it; the results spoke for themselves. The workers had given their support when asked, helping to turn the loss at Bressay in 1979 into profit during 1980. There was no problem with the fact that this would be the last year of a Christmas bonus, but to withdraw this expected payment at the eleventh hour was like a slap in the face. After a lengthy discussion, I finally won the day. The Bressay workers got their Christmas bonus, knowing that it would be their last, and accepted the inevitable.

The flimsy, cement-asbestos sheeting on the meal store was forever getting broken, as pallets of meal were moved about. Replacing broken sheets had become an on-going task. In frustration, I decided that the only solution was to replace the sheeting with a concrete block wall. It would be a simple matter to build concrete blocks in between the existing steel beams.

Explaining on the phone to MD Ian Hughes what I had in mind, he agreed. Our capable workers built thousands of concrete blocks, and by spring 1981 the job was done.

When Ian came on a visit in August 1981, he was very impressed to see the finished work, especially since it had been done by our own employees.

Several days later, he called to say that he had told Christian about the fine job that we had done, and that Christian had said to do the same with the factory.

"That, I will not do," I said. "It would be crazy. The building has stood there for 100 years, and is in a state of collapse. The foundations are not capable of supporting a block wall. It just isn't on to upgrade that old building."

Ian was taken aback by my outburst and passed little comment. Soon after he was back on the phone again, saying that he had passed on my comments to Christian. "What was the reaction?

"You and I have to go to Bergen for a meeting; that's what he said."

Two weeks later (September 1981) Ian and I were met at Bergen airport by Bjørn Skulstad now the company's project engineer and, incidentally, my skiing instructor from 1965. Our first stop was at a factory where pre-cast elements were manufactured. On seeing a complete building, I thought: This is just what is required at Heogan.

We then drove to Bergen to meet Christian, who welcomed us in his usual jovial manner. Thinking that perhaps there would be some convincing to do, I had prepared a report stating my views regarding the future of the process building. Handing out copies to those present, I asked if they would read it before the meeting started.

It had taken a week to prepare the lengthy report, which showed in detail why it was imperative to build a new factory, as opposed to refurbishing the old. The machinery installation in the existing factory was far from ideal. To remove the rotor from a drier for maintenance or repair would entail removing the entire evaporator plant, to gain access. The list of disadvantages against refurbishing was extensive, not least the timescale and disruption to production. The target timescale, for completion of the proposed factory, with all machinery in place, was April 1983.

Christian read every word, and then laid the report on the table. He shook me by his only comment. He simply said: "OK, we'll build it!"

Wheels were set in motion at full speed. There was much to do, but Bjørn and I had two small problems to sort out. Bjørn had arranged to start up a new evaporation plant on St Pierre, an island near the coast of Newfoundland. With his work load of designing the new layout for Bressay, he would be hard pushed for time. Would I take on to do the work on St Pierre? They spoke only French on the island, but not to worry, an American translator would be at hand. To me it sounded a daunting task, and I was delighted when informed that, due to lack of fish, the trip was cancelled.

Our second problem was that Bjarnhild and I had planned to visit relations in New Zealand in December 1982, and there was no way that I was going to cancel that trip for a second time. Bjørn agreed to take over at Heogan in my absence.

Soon after Ian's visit in August 1981, I got a phone call from him asking if there was any quick way that we could try an experiment with storage of meal in bulk. (Perhaps the new concrete block walls of the meal store had been an inspiration).

As the meal was conveyed pneumatically through a sectional 5 inch pipe, joined by quick release couplings; it was a simple matter to divert the pipework from the day silo directly into the meal store.

To assist cooling, it was necessary to distribute the meal throughout the building. For that purpose a high level catwalk was required through the length of the building. Sandy and Rune constructed the catwalk, and when it was complete, the pipeline was supported on top. It was then a simple task for one man to disconnect the pipe at any given point and, by attaching a short bend, distribute the meal where desired. Thirty one years on, the system is still in use, unchanged.

While working on the installation, Rune narrowly escaped a nasty accident. He had been working from a pallet, suspended on a forklift, some 20ft above ground level. When someone requested to borrow the forklift for a few minutes, Rune stepped onto the catwalk. As he did so a hydraulic hose burst, and the forklift mast and pallet dropped like a stone.

Now at last, dreams of building a new factory had become a reality. Frank Johnston was recalled with his digger and bulldozer, and over a period of several weeks thousands of tons of clay and mud were pushed seawards. The excavations were more extensive than had been envisaged, but the end result was a good firm base on which to build.

Maurice Anderson was the driving force behind the foundation building of the new factory, and was a great asset during that hectic time. Growing up on a croft, Maurice was well used to manual work from an early age. He had started work in the office at Heogan in 1968, when he left school at 16. He was competent and reliable, doing the office work for 10 years, until taking on the responsibilities of assistant manager in 1978.

During the construction period he was in his element, out working among the boys and setting the pace to keep the work going. If I asked him to do something in the office, it was promptly done and like a flash he was out among the boys again.

Foundations for this type of building had to be exact to ensure that the wall and roof elements would fit properly. Olav Dyngeland, a retired builder with much experience in that type of work, was sent over from Bergen to control all measurements and levels.

There were some hilarious episodes with Olav, who didn't speak a word of English, but spoke nonstop in his own language hoping that some of what he said would be understood by the locals. He frequently needed assistance to get his message across, but there was a limit as to how much time I could spend with him. One day while I was helping him check some measurements he said: "Hold on a minute, we have an Englishman here." That was the first time that I had heard a twist in a tape referred to as an 'Englishman'.

Olav had been out attempting to do some measurements on a very windy morning. It was very important to get this one spot on he said, but the wind was playing havoc, and he described the tape going in the shape of a rainbow. I said that I would help him, but first I must make some phone calls. So off he went to the site once more. I still hadn't finished my phone calls when he was back with a huge grin on his face, declaring: "I got it"

"What have you got Olav?"

"Oh, I just weighed the tape down with some planks." He said with another grin.

Work on the site stopped over the Christmas and New Year period (1981/82). Olav and I were asked to give a progress report at a pre-Christmas meeting in Bergen. The invitation included Bjarnhild, so we had a fine Christmas in Norway at the company's expense.

At the meeting, Olav was enthusiastic about progress made, but just as I expected he had to throw in some adverse comment about Shetland's weather, with emphasis on the wind. The wind in Shetland blew nonstop, he declared. He had never experienced anything like it. When you were out walking, you had to lean forward at an angle of 45 degrees. If the wind stopped suddenly, you would have gone flat on your face, said Olav, to the great amusement of the meeting.

THE 1980S – PART TWO

IN SPITE of adverse weather, the foundations were completed on time, and in due course the prefabricated building elements arrived at the Norscot base in Lerwick. Transportation to Bressay had become so much easier with the arrival of the inter-island car ferries in 1975. Heavy lifts were now handled in a completely different way than in 1968 and 1971.

The roof elements were the heaviest items, weighing 18 tonnes each, and were 24 metres in length. Two of Larry Sutherland's trailers of 40ft and 30ft were welded together to carry them one by one. But first some corners on the very narrow Heogan road had to be upgraded.

Thanks to the skill of its driver, the massive heavy lift mobile crane made the precarious journey from Maryfield to Heogan and back safely, at times with only half of the wheel width supported on the tarmac.

MV Grima *arrives with a roof section for the new factory.* Rune Tulloch

'Lowrie' towing a 70 foot trailer. Rune Tulloch

A long trailer, on a sharp bend. *Rune Tulloch*

The big crane. *Rune Tulloch*

The first section on end.
Rune Tulloch *Agile as cats.* *Rune Tulloch*

A team of builders from the Norwegian manufacturers N.O.B.I. erected the building without a hitch during the spring / summer of 1982, thanks no doubt to Olav Dyngeland's care and attention to the foundations. The new factory was a milestone in the Heogan story, ensuring a stable and more secure future for the island.

During the autumn, we were making plans for our long awaited trip to New Zealand. As arranged I was relying on Bjørn to take over in my absence. I was therefore very surprised when he called to say that he had decided to move to the USA, where he would establish his own company, trading within the fish meal and

Inside the factory.
Dennis Coutts

The author in front of the newly completed factory, 1983.   *Dennis Coutts*

Aerial view during the 1980s.   *Dennis Coutts*

oil industry. Luckily he had completed the layout drawings, which looked good.

Regarding someone to oversee the machinery installation, Bjørn recommend Inge Kolltveit, who I was assured was very capable. I had met Inge back in July1972, when he and a colleague came over from Bergen to do an efficiency test on a drier. Their visit coincided with our house-warming party. Inge said recently that he remembers very well arriving at the party, but strangely, has no recollection of going back to the hotel.

To ensure that everything was under control, I documented everything that I could think of for Inge and Maurice. When we left for our travels in early December 1982, I was confident that the project was in safe hands.

After a fantastic trip to New Zealand we returned to a hive of activity. Work at the factory was going full swing, and our house was occupied by the Norwegian workers. One of them had brought his wife as housekeeper, so everything was ship shape.

The old factory closed down in September 1982. After relocating all usable machinery, it looked as if it had been hit by a bomb. The machinery layout in the old factory had left much to be desired and I was looking forward to seeing a properly designed layout in the new building.

Production in the new building started on target in April 1983, and the remnants of the old building were cleared from the site at the end of the sand eel season, in September 1983.

Salmon farming was now getting a foothold in Shetland, and led to the formation of 50 small companies. George Reid had had a negative attitude towards salmon farming, saying that it had no future. With a change of company directors, things were seen in a more positive light. A suggested experimental unit at the Freshers pier did not meet with my approval, but a pilot project in Aiths Voe on Bressay was seriously considered.

I was invited to see an experimental unit in Norway, where salmon were reared in a lagoon. It was an interesting concept, but impractical, and was short lived.

HBP had built a salmon hatchery in the Western Isles, and there was interest in doing likewise in Shetland. I spent many days roaming around Shetland looking for a potential hatchery site, and eventually recommended one at East Burrafirth. An objection by a local resident put paid to the proposed development. It had been an interesting project, but I was not unduly concerned to see it dropped.

The main ingredients in salmon feed are fish meal and oil. It was therefore logical to produce salmon feed at Heogan. The fish meal and oil factory at Fuglafjord in the Faroe Islands were already doing it, so why not do it at Heogan? The Aberdeen directors liked the idea and suggested that I should do some research.

Two new boats for the Shetland fishing fleet arrive at Lerwick Harbour on the same day, Altaire *and* Diamond, *1987.* Robert Johnson

I had not yet been in Faroe, but had spoken many times on the telephone with company director Eldøy. On expressing an interest of visiting their factory, Eldøy said that he would be pleased to meet me and show me around.

Hearing what I had arranged, our directors decided to charter a small plane, as they would also like to see the factory. And so a deputation of five people made the journey.

Director Eldøy was very polite and escorted us on brief tour of the factory. We were then ushered to the board room for coffee and given a talk about the company's activities. It had become obvious, however, that we were looked upon as potential competitors regarding the salmon feed plant.

We were invited to dinner at the local hotel where we were escorted into a private dining room. When we were seated Eldøy opened his large briefcase, and to our amusement, it didn't hold any paper or documents – it contained only bottles of spirits. Faroe was dry at that time and this was an acceptable way of bending the rules.

After sampling the contents of the briefcase and with a good meal under our belts, it was time to head back to our waiting plane. A bank of fog was rolling in towards the airport and we were all relieved to be airborne and heading for home. Nevertheless it had been a memorable occasion, even if it had not been the most successful of business trips.

I was not going to be put off by one small obstacle, however. Knowing that the salmon feed plant was made in Denmark, I made several enquiries by phone, and eventually got through to the manufacturers. They were good sales people, offering to give assistance wherever necessary. Had I seen their plant in Iceland? A trip there could easily be arranged.

After considering at length, the company directors decided to drop the project. Our main outlet for fish meal and oil was to salmon feed manufacturers, and it was decided that we could not take the risk of losing markets by going into direct competition with our customers. Perhaps more thought should have been given to that point at the outset.

Having set my mind on the development, I had been assuring Shetland fish farmers that we were going to manufacture fish feed at Heogan, and it went against the grain to go back on my word. But there comes a time to back off.

I had known Gibby Johnston for a long time. He was a man with drive and ambition who had done much towards developing Shetlands white fish industry. With assistance from the Highlands and Islands Development Board, he had been instrumental in setting up filleting factories throughout Shetland. He was now into salmon farming in a big way, and we had had numerous discussions regarding salmon feed.

One day I got a call from Gibby, asking if I knew that Andy Jackson from Fulmar was in Shetland. Andy was looking for an agent to sell salmon feed locally. Would I be interested? As I was still smarting over the dropped plans to manufacture at Heogan I said yes, I would be interested.

Following a meeting with the Fulmar salesman, Bjarnhild and I went to Norfolk where we saw the feed mill, met the team, and signed an agency agreement.

Bjarnhild had tried her hand at various things in Shetland; she had worked as a telephonist in the Lerwick exchange, had worked in a drapers shop, had done relief work at the Norwegian Welfare Centre and had done bed and breakfast from home. Serious thought had been given to building a hotel on Bressay, but raising capital was the stumbling block.

During her years in Shetland, she had observed a strong local interest for Norway. Five hundred years of Scottish rule had not dampened the local feeling towards Norway. Even though there was no direct passenger link at that time, Bergen was no further away than Aberdeen. Shetlanders in general did not look on Norwegians as foreigners. Even if the dialect has been very much diluted there are still a lot of Norse words in use. One glance at the map is enough to confirm where the names had originated.

Bjarnhild saw an opportunity to provide Scandinavian furniture as an alternative to that available in Lerwick shops, giving a great opportunity for a small business. In the summer of 1983, she and her father went on holiday to Norway and came back laden with catalogues and samples in addition to some new furniture. An advert was put in the *Shetland Times* and the furniture sold immediately. In 1984 along with Rune and his wife Fiona, we started our family business, Tulloch Enterprises. The furniture sales took off, and the business became very interesting.

Working at Heogan during the week, and in our own business at the weekend was very demanding. I started to think that it was time to move on.

In the spring of 1986 I tendered my resignation, giving my employers six months notice. Christian was not happy to hear the news. He called me by phone, asking if I was sure that this was what I really wanted to do. I have forgotten what my answer was, but I'm sure it was not easy to say how I felt. He was a fantastic man, and for me it had been a great privilege to have known him during my years at Heogan.

Looking back, I realise that HBP had been a fantastic company to work for. With little education, I had got the opportunity to do many things that I would not have had elsewhere.

In October 1986, Bjarnhild and I were invited by the company directors to attend a private dinner party in an Aberdeen hotel. Christian had come over especially for the occasion. After the meal he had a few words to say and then presented me with a gift. It was a hand-made silver Viking ship mounted on a hard wood stand, with an inscription plate acknowledging 31years faithful service. The model was of the Oseberg ship, dating back to 820AD. It was found in 1904, in a buried mound in Slagen, Vestfold, south west of Oslo. The ship measured 21.5 metres long with 5 metres beam. It had been manned by 15 pairs of oars and its mast was 9 metres high. Remains of a woman, who must have been of high status, were found buried in the ship. As Christian handed over my present he said: "You wouldn't be able to buy that one in a shop."

It was just like him, one of a kind.

On 24th September 1987, I got a call from Ian Hughes' son with the sad news that his father had died. Towards the end he had asked for pen and paper, writing down five names and said: "That's the boys that I want to be at my funeral."

I was honoured to be there. We had become good friends during his many trips to Heogan and I have many pleasant memories of him.

In early 1989 I heard that Christian was unwell, and called his son Sigfinn, to enquire about his father. It was just a matter of time I was told: "Is he able to speak on the phone?" I asked.

Sigfinn said that the best time to call was in the afternoon. Christian was very pleased to get my call, saying that he really would have liked to see Shetland one more time, but that it was now too late. About six weeks later I attended his funeral in Bergen, to pay my respects to a very special man.

The company directors chartered a small plane, to fly to Bergen for the funeral. I was invited to join them, and George Reid, who had by then retired, was there also. With his long standing involvement with Christian, it was not surprising to see him at the funeral. I had not seen George for some years and it was good to meet up again and to discuss things from the past.

Our pilot had arranged some refreshments for the return flight to Aberdeen. Miniature whiskies were handed round, and George managed to polish off five during the journey. By the time he stepped onto the tarmac in Aberdeen he had become quite jovial and announced: "Well boys, I really enjoyed that. That is of course, if it's possible to enjoy a funeral."

George lived alone in Aberdeen for some time following his wife's death, and eventually moved to Melton Mowbray, to be near his daughter. One day, I got a phone call from Magnie Shearer to say that George Reid had died. I sent a letter of condolence to his daughter, expressing what her father had meant to me; how it was he who had persuaded me to accept a challenge in 1964, and had been there with assurance and support when I needed it.

Two days later, I got a phone call from George's son in law. He had been asked to speak at the funeral, but was at a loss to know what to say. He knew so little about what George had done in his working life. Could he read my letter at the funeral? I was pleased to give my consent. It was good to know that my letter was, in some small way, a tribute to the fine man who had been my boss, but had also become a friend.

15

BARRA

I THOUGHT I had finished with fish meal factories, but in December 1986 I got a surprise phone call from Helge Hovland, then vice-chairman of the HBP Board. The company had recently taken over Hull Fishmeal Company, and a factory on the island of Barra. They had a problem at Barra, however. The factory had not operated for some time and was in need of renovation. Would I be interested in helping to get it going again?

Before I had time to say no, Helge threw in what was on offer; double my previous salary with the company and all expenses paid. I replied that I would need to see first-hand what was involved.

Three days later, Helge and I made a recognisance trip to Barra. To say that it needed some renovation was an understatement. But I saw it as a challenge, and decided to have a go.

Setting out in early January 1987, I picked up a firm's car in Aberdeen and drove to Oban to catch Caledonian MacBrayne's ferry for the six hour crossing to Barra. As it was snowing when I left Aberdeen, I was a bit apprehensive about road conditions. I had good protective clothing, and as a precaution, bought a tow rope and a plastic shovel. All went well and I arrived in Castle Bay on a Saturday. On Sunday I drove to the factory to take stock. Standing there alone I thought: what am I doing here? Have I taken leave of my senses? I should be home in Bressay. But I had given my word, and there was no turning back.

It soon became apparent that the problems at Barra were bigger than envisaged. The Highlands and Islands Development Board had built the factory and pier at Ardvenish, North Bay, and had leased it to Hull

Fishmeal Company. Two salmon farms, one on either side of the relatively narrow sea loch, had also got funding from HIDB. It was a recipe for disaster from the start. Any effluent discharged from the factory would pass through the fish farms.

Jeff Smith, the manager from Hull, spent the first three days with me to show me the ropes and how things 'should' work. The factory building, meal store, boiler room and pier were all fine, as was the office, workers canteen, toilets and showers. A fish handling pump, fish storage silo and conveyor system had all been new when installed, as were fuel tanks and fish oil tanks. The diesel fired steam boiler was also in good working order. But there, the positive ended.

The process machinery was mainly cast offs from Hull and the layout plan and installation was poor. As Jeff and I were going through the factory I was passing adverse remarks as they became apparent. Suddenly Jeff stopped and turned to me in frustration: "You have done nothing but criticise since we stepped inside that door."

"Well tell me then, who designed this place?"

Jeff looked at me, rather sheepishly: "I did."

What could one say to that, except, "Oh."

He broke the ice by saying: "I wish you had been here when I designed it, it might have been done a bit better".

Following that initial outburst I stopped criticising; there was no point. It was just to get stuck in and sort things out.

Helge called to enquire how things were going, and got a verbal report. He expected the factory to be operational within two months.

"That is impossible," he was told. "But three months is realistic. To achieve that, it will be necessary to hire in some skilled labour, and it will involve working long hours."

"Just do your best, and get the place operational as soon as possible," was his final remark. I never heard from him again and he died soon afterwards.

Gordon Wilson was the young company director given responsibility for the Barra investment. I had known Gordon since 1968. He had started to work for the company after leaving school. Working his way up, he was promoted to director in the 1980s. During the refurbishing period, Gordon made frequent trips to Barra, flying from Glasgow with Logan Air to land when the tide was out on that great expanse of sand, known as Barra Airport.

On Gordon's first visit, he and I were called to a crises meeting with the two local salmon farmers. They were very concerned at the prospect of the factory going back into production, and were seeking assurance that no effluent would be discharged from the factory.

To give such an assurance was impossible; it was not realistic to operate the factory with zero effluent discharge. We would do everything possible to keep the discharge under control, but would give no guarantee against a situation resulting in losses of fish on their farms.

Gordon and I agreed on my work schedule. I would do three week work periods, followed by one week free to go home. Initially I took the Logan air flight from Barra to Glasgow, hired a self-drive car and drove to Aberdeen to catch the flight to Sumburgh. As the flights did not connect, I had to spend one night in the Glasgow airport hotel on the return journey. After several trips home in this round about fashion, I discovered a more direct route. British Airways had a flight starting from Benbecula, Uist, via Inverness, Kirkwall and onward to Sumburgh. This was much more convenient and time saving.

I don't know the circumstances leading to the closure of the Barra factory, but when production stopped, the machinery had been left unwashed. It was crawling with maggots and millions of small flies, the likes of which I had never seen in Shetland. My first priority was therefore to get the place cleaned up.

I called the Aberdeen office, requesting two things from Bressay that would be invaluable at Barra. The first was a powerful high pressure washer. The second: Could I borrow Sandy Lippe for three months? Both requests were granted, and both proved equally effective.

The company had reinstated the former workforce, and I soon discovered that they were a pleasant bunch, willing and enthusiastic to see some all-round changes and improvements. Many defects came to light in the factory. Of some 400 tubes in the three stage evaporation plant, 90% were blocked. When the pressure washer from Bressay arrived, I put on an oilskin suit and tackled the job of clearing the tubes. Hugh Sinclair, who was foreman, passed a comment: "This is not really your job, is it?"

"Oh, what do you do you think my job is then?"

"Should you not be in the office?"

I made my intentions quite clear. My role was to get the factory operational and I had no intention of sitting in the office. We worked well together; the fact that I was a fellow islander had perhaps something to say.

The press would definitely have to be dismantled for cleaning, but no provision had been made for lifting the top section, weighing two tons. Sandy's first priority was therefore to construct a gantry and lifting tackle for the purpose; but first the necessary steelwork had to be ordered from Brown & Tawse in Glasgow, a very reliable firm which I had used much in the past.

Virtually nothing mechanical could be purchased on the island; all materials and supplies had to be ordered from Glasgow and transported via Oban on the ferry, or sometimes by Logan Air, depending on the urgency. Once, in a crisis, I chartered Logan Air to deliver an electric motor.

Practical thought had been lacking, regarding the installation of the upright production tanks, which stood directly on the floor. The flow pipes were fitted some 70cm from the bottom. No provision had been made for drainage. The same design had been used on the fish oil tanks. I could hardly believe my eyes.

By improvising, a false bottom of stones and shingle was formed, with a finishing layer of smooth concrete, sloping towards a drainage valve. The end result was effective and hygienic; making cleaning of all tanks an easy task.

At Bressay we had used the Glasgow Company, Centraforce to do a yearly service on the oil separators. I was on friendly terms with the owners, Alan Crawford and Bill Garret. It was therefore logical to ask them to do a service at Barra. Bill flew from Glasgow to do the service. It was good to meet again and we had much to talk about. He enquired about my father and somehow the conversation turned to something that father had spoken about so many times. It was Orange Grove rum. If I ever came across it, would I buy a bottle for him? It was my grandfather's favourite, I had been told.

Bill had never seen or heard of that brand of rum, but would keep his eye going he promised. Not long after his return to Glasgow, I got a call from Loganair. A parcel was there for me to collect.

I opened the parcel having no idea what to expect. To my surprise, it was a bottle of Orange Grove rum. Father, then 81, was delighted with his present and the bottle was promptly opened so that we could both have a taste.

Safety at Barra had been of low priority and guards were virtually non-existent. A high level platform had holes in the metalwork, large enough for a man to fall through. Had a factory inspector dropped in, the factory would immediately have been closed down. I vowed that the wheels would not turn again until the factory was made safe.

The work list was growing by the day, and the renovation work was soon going full swing. The team of willing workers were fantastic, doing a minimum 12 hour day. The time just flew past and I was enjoying the experience.

The majority of people on Barra are Catholics, a marked contrast to Lewis & Harris where the protestant faith is predominant. Knowing the aversion to Sunday work in Stornaway, I enquired what was acceptable in Barra. Sunday working was quite acceptable it was stated, but it was imperative to have one hour free either on Saturday or Sunday in order to attend mass.

HBP owned a similar factory in Stornaway, where Sunday work was banned. I was in for severe criticism one Monday morning while on the phone to the Stornaway factory manager. When I referred to how well things had gone at Barra on Sunday, he exploded: "You are just a bunch of heathens; they were bad enough there before you got in among them!"

The Barra men spoke Gaelic among themselves, but out of politeness the conversation was always in English when I was present. Consequently I learned little of their language during the eleven months spent there. They sometimes listened to a Gaelic broadcast from Ireland on the radio, comparing the difference between Irish and Scottish Gaelic. To me it all sounded equally difficult.

One day I heard shouts and commotion in the factory followed by: "Where's the Sheltie?"

I had previously heard of the elderly crofter who frequently drove to factory on his tractor to get his tank topped up with diesel. He had sailed with Shetlanders in his young day and was full of enthusiasm from that time.

Referring to his Shetland shipmates he exclaimed: "Man, those boys were tough; they never felt the heat or the cold."

The old man's visit lightened my day.

Two fitters were hired in from an engineering works in Huntly; another two were sent from the Fraserburgh factory to help out. One was Sandy Taylor. He was a good hand and very versatile. One day I gave him a printed work list, retaining a copy for reference. There were 12 items on the list, and for good measure I had added item number 13.

Sandy started walking away as he read the list, and when he reached the bottom, turned and came back laughing: "I really like item 13 best."

Item number 13 was: "Come back for a new list."

We had a lot of fun to lighten the mood, and there was a good atmosphere all round. One day, while discussing the workload with one of the locals, I said: "Oh well, Rome wasn't built in a day."

"That's because you weren't gaffer on the job," was the answer.

One day, when Sandy Lippe was doing a job, he said in frustration: "I wish I had an anvil here."

Next day while on the phone to Brown & Tawse I enquired: "You wouldn't by any chance have an anvil?"

The store-man laughed as he said: "Well it's not one of our best-selling lines nowadays, but there's one in the store which has stood there for years."

And so, to Sandy's delight, he got his anvil, but was also in for some teasing about the potential of shodding horses on Barra.

The 14 mile ring road on Barra follows the shoreline round the island. Initially we stayed in a hotel in Castle Bay, some seven miles away from the factory. I therefore made a point of circling the island each day. Barra is a beautiful island with a profusion of wild flowers in summer. It is known as 'The garden of the Hebrides'. I went waking a lot, enjoying the tranquillity of the island. One day I climbed the mountain above Castle Bay. From its summit the view was fantastic. Looking around at the huge stone boulders strewn everywhere I thought to myself: 'There has been some upheaval here'. It was interesting to discover that the mountain was named 'The Hevil'.

After some time, Sandy got a caravan sited at the factory and I moved to the Isle of Barra Hotel, an arrangement which suited us both. When the hotel closed for the winter, I hired the manager's flat in the hotel which involved some personal effort doing self-catering, but I liked the arrangement much better. Bjarnhild had been visiting her sister in Sweden in May and on return, came to stay with me on Barra. It was great to see her and the dinner menu got a great boost. We flew up to Faro for ten days, before returning to Shetland. Then it was back to Barra once more. It had been a fantastic break from work.

After three months, there was still much work to do, but the factory was now in a much better shape. I informed the directors that we were ready to start production. Several days later the first cargo arrived and from then on, the factory was working round the clock.

There was one item of machinery that I was concerned about, but time had not permitted to do anything about it, furthermore I had not found a solution to the problem. A vertical conveyor some 10 metres in length, similar to the vertical fish unloader at Heogan, elevated the fish from the silo. From there, a 'cast off' twin screw conveyor from Hull had been utilised to convey fish to the cooker. The twin screws ran in a square box, elevated at an angle of 15 degrees. This design had probably served its purpose at Hull, where the raw material was whitefish offal. But it was completely unsuitable for conveying small fish.

The first load of sand eels arrived, just as I was about to leave the factory for a week at home, I knew that we were in trouble but kept the thought to myself. When Bjarnhild met me at Sumburgh I told her it was unlikely that I would be home for a week this time. As expected, the phone was ringing as soon as we stepped inside our door. Ian Kemp, who had been left in charge, was on the phone. "We have a problem" he announced.

"I know you do, you cannot get any fish into the cooker."

He confirmed that that was indeed the problem. He was assured that I would be back on Monday.

Sitting on the plane on Monday morning pondering the problem, the answer suddenly dawned on me; we would simply use cement. When the plane landed at Glasgow, I called Ian, asking if quick set cement was available on the island. He said that we could buy ordinary cement from a local builder, and was told to order some; I would buy an additive in Glasgow. On getting instructions to empty the conveyor and clean it thoroughly, he asked what I had in mind. "We will use cement to fill the gaps".

"We can make some moulds till you arrive" said Ian.

"Just ensure that the conveyor is thoroughly clean. That's all you have to do."

After welding in some short stubs of reinforcing bar we simply threw in a batch of quick set cement, started the conveyor and got two perfectly formed tunnels. The screws were turned occasionally as the cement set, and another problem had been solved. It ran like that for the duration of the factory.

Sometimes it becomes necessary to improvise, or take strong measures to get things moving. Late one night a bearing collapsed on a fish conveyor bringing production to a standstill. Two fitters worked all night attempting to extract a chain sprocket, which refused to budge. Early next morning, to the horror of one of the fitters who had worked all night, they were told: "Take a burner and cut through that shaft, replace the bearing and then weld the shaft back; I don't care if it wobbles, just get it done."

It ran in a haphazard fashion until time permitted to replace the shaft.

When discharging boats, water was required to assist the fish pump. In order to cut down on the effluent discharge, the contaminated water was retained in a tank to be used on the next cargo. It was a bad idea which would lead to problems.

One day it became necessary to discharge the stale water into the sea, as it had stood too long and could not be recycled. The ebbing tide carried the discharge right through both fish farms, resulting in a considerable loss of fish. The owners were, not surprisingly, hopping mad. However, a financial settlement was reached between the insurers and H.B.P. and the incident was buried along with the fish.

An encounter with carbon monoxide gases almost led to tragedy at Barra.

A Faroese crew had delivered their catch at the factory. Three days later they were back with a full load of fresh fish. When the fish silo was filled to capacity, there was still a considerable amount left in the ships hold.

Meanwhile, an oil tanker was waiting to deliver fuel oil. I spoke to the fishing skipper, asking if he would kindly vacate the berth. He agreed and took his boat out to sea. He then decided to fly home to Faro for the weekend. Several days later he was alongside at Ardvinish to finish discharging. I was in the office when a young employee rushed in; announcing that one of the boys has fallen in the hold and hit his head.

From that I deducted that the man had fallen into the hold. I knew that Ian Kemp had recently attended a first aid course, and instructed the young man to find Ian and get him to the boat as fast as possible.

Ian was close behind me as I went down a ladder, into the hold. A big man lay face down at my feet, his face buried in fish. Another stood by, swaying on his feet, on the verge of to collapse. One look into his eyes told me the cause, it was gas. The gas had formed, not from the fish, but from the recycled water. Four men sat among the fish, further in through the hold. Bending down, I lifted the unconscious man, and Ian, wiping fish and grime from his face, confirming: "He's all right, he's still breathing."

The gas was obviously more intense at the bottom of the hold and by stooping to assist the victim; I got the full impact and went out like a light.

For what happened next, I and several others owe our lives to the brave action of Hugh Sinclair, the factory foreman. He was lowered by the ships crane into the hold in a brail (landing net) suspended on a wire rope. As Hugh grabbed me and hauled me into the brail, I started to come round and was aware of him also hauling Ian to safety. Poor Ian was given a kick for good measure as he was told: "Don't you damned well pass out as well."

Hugh went back in the brail and eventually got everyone to safety. I lay on the deck, violently sick and only partially conscious. When attempting to climb the ladder, someone restrained me, saying to take it easy. When I eventually stepped onto the pier, Gordon Wilson stood there, white faced and shaken. I remember his exact words: "Oh Hebbie Tulloch, I thought we had lost you."

It was by sheer coincidence that Gordon had arrived from Aberdeen that day. I showered and put on clean clothes which I kept in the car.

Gordon told me that he was going to drive to Castle Bay, to get some disinfectant for the ships hold and I decided to accompany him. On the fourteen mile round trip, he had to stop three times to allow me out to be sick at the roadside. I was told in no uncertain terms that the next day would be a holiday for me. I didn't argue.

Next morning after a late breakfast, I went for a walk. As I went past the Catholic Church in Castle Bay, I suddenly got an urge to go inside. Sitting there alone, many thoughts and visions came to me. How different the outcome could have been with the unthinkable possibility of arriving at the factory to find six men dead in the hold of a Faroese fishing boat. That day I thanked God, and Hugh Sinclair, for saving our lives.

About that time a similar situation occurred at Heogan, when Ronald Henderson and Laurence Manson were overcome by lethal fumes in the pits. Manager Mike Tippen was able to save them by climbing down a ladder with ropes. The victims were quite badly affected and spent several days recovering in hospital.

Much worse was the fatal accident onboard a Danish fishing boat. They had been sheltering in Lerwick for some days, with a mixed cargo of industrial and edible fish on board. Shortly after the boat left Lerwick, one of the three man crew went into the hold to check the cargo. He did not return.

A second man went to investigate and did not return either. The skipper turned the boat and steamed back to Lerwick, arriving too late. Both men were dead, killed by the lethal gas.

During my stay in Barra I constantly carried my camera in the car and got some good photos. I have a mania for unusual stones and when I find something interesting, it is added to my collection. One Sunday, while staying in the rented flat, I went for a walk on the long sandy beach below the hotel. As the tide was out I was exploring among the rocks, hoping to find a keepsake from Barra.

Looking down, a beautiful stone lay at my feet; it definitely was not a local stone. My guess is that it had been carried there thousands of years ago in a receding ice age. While walking in the rocky interior, I had observed huge scores in the rocks all pointing in a south westerly direction. Perhaps this stone had left its mark somewhere as it was carried by the moving ice. I took the stone back to the flat and laid it on the floor in front of the TV, surprised to see it reflect the light.

My contract at Barra finished at the end of November 1987. It had been a great experience and rewarding to see the factory functional and back in production again.

When I packed my suitcase, the nine kilo stone was included. There was no way that I was going to leave that fine stone behind. Amazingly, I was not asked to pay excess baggage, but on arriving back in Bressay someone lifted my suitcase and asked: "Whit does do hae in dis case, stones?"

Just before Christmas that year I was surprised and honoured to get a present of a pewter tankard inscribed: HERBIE. From The Boys On Barra, December '87.

Sadly, as HBP was winding down, the Barra factory was the first to close. One day some time later, I saw a familiar sight at Heogan. It was three tanks which had been cut in two to reduce weight for transport. When I looked inside, amazingly, all three had been delivered complete with stones and concrete from Barra.

16

SALMON FARMING IN SHETLAND

THE pioneers of Shetland's salmon farming were namely, John White, Gibby Johnston, and August Alfredson, with Jim Scott and Alistair Goodlad close behind. Soon every Voe and Bay in Shetland was being looked at as a potential site.

While working on Barra, I was still acting as agent for a salmon feed company, but the business was just ticking over. Fulmar feed was high quality and the fish growth rate was good, but 10% dust in the feed dampened the enthusiasm of our customers. I attended a salmon farming conference/exhibition in Inverness in 1987. Two weary days on the Fulmar stand had been enough, and on the final day I took my leave and went exploring. I looked with some interest at pump ashore stations but realised that the capital investment would be enormous.

Something caught my eye. It was a scale model of an octagonal plastic salmon cage, complete with timber walkway. Waiting till the coast was clear, I made contact with the Norwegian salesman, Erling Sandøy. He was very enthusiastic about his product and hinted that they were looking for a local agent. Later that summer Erling came to visit us in Bressay with an offer of an agency on commission basis. We accepted, and Tulloch Enterprises became Preplast's agent for Scotland.

My work in Barra was finished in November 1987. Changes in fire law regulations in 1988 were making a future in Scandinavian furniture sales look less than promising. A change of direction was again called for. When I expressed an interest in salmon farming, Bjarnhild's only comment was: "What are you waiting for?"

I have always loved the sea and boats, and hens had always held a fascination for me. It would be like feeding hens in the sea I mused.

Aith Voe was a small, potential site on the east side of Bressay. It was sheltered but very shallow, with only 6.7 metres water depth at low tide. It could, however, be an ideal starting point.

I contacted Lerwick Harbour Trust (the controlling authority for Aiths Voe) expressing interest to farm salmon in the Voe. It transpired that John and Alistair Goodlad had also made moves in the same direction.

The outcome was that in early 1988, the three of us got together to form the company Bressay Salmon Ltd. It was a good and successful arrangement. I became the major shareholder and managing director but it was hands on from the outset. Our board meetings were few and very casual.

As a rule, cash flows and funding was John's department, while practical issues were discussed with Alistair.

Angie Mackechnie was our first employee. He and I serviced the site in a Voe Boat, from the beach at Globa. Angie was a native of the island of Jura. He was a character, but a good worker and very reliable. I knew him well from his time of employment at Heogan. Angie and Mary stayed at Bruntland within walking distance of the site. She was delighted when he became our first employee and said that the bonus was that Angie did not have to pass a pub on his way home from work.

We started small and never became a large producer; our annual smolt input topping at 100,000 in 1998. Circumstances determined, however, that the company's initial growth came faster than planned. We had one 70 metre cage in the sea and had chartered a Whalsay fishing boat to deliver 5,000 smolts. Aith Voe is a basin with a shallow entrance. The boats draft was too deep to cross the shallow ridge, and it was agreed that they would lie at anchor while we transported the smolts in a Voe Boat. A suitable transport tank was borrowed from Skerries Salmon Ltd.

The first tank delivery went without a hitch, but as we motored out the Voe the seagulls were having a field day from the water around the boat. It transpired that a grating in the bottom of the hold had come loose and that our precious fish

Mary and Angie McKechnie. Mary worked in the canteen for some time.

Bressay Heritage Centre

138

were being pumped over the side. We had no idea how many smolts had been lost and decided to order 5,000 replacements. All went well on the second delivery and our initial loss was less than expected.

The following year we ordered 20,000 smolts. Our contract stated that the smolts would be 45 to 50 grams each. The Well Boat was due to deliver to Alistair's farm at Trondra, before making the Bressay delivery. Late on a Friday night, I got a phone call from Alistair. On hearing that the Well Boat had arrived with 38 gram average fish, I refused to take delivery. The outcome was that Alistair bought the cargo at a rock bottom price and an order was placed elsewhere for Bressay Salmon.

In 1990 we acquired a second site in Dales Voe, again at courtesy of Lerwick Harbour Trust. It was a much better site, with deeper water and a better water exchange. We put 60,000 smolts onto the new site. It became necessary to employ more regular employees. John Rognaldsen, who then lived in Whalsay, was employed as skipper when we bought MV *Sjoglimt* II from Norway in March 1989.

I had not finished my contact with Heogan, however. The then disused Heogan factory pier became our shore base together with a shore site close to the factory. From then on, we kept our boats at Heogan and operated from there during my time in salmon farming.

John Rognaldsen's son, Kevin, was our next regular employee, followed in turn by Douglas Scollay, Jamie Grunberg and Torbjørn Riise. Douglas became very good at plastic welding and spent most of his time repairing the octagonal plastic cages, a never ending task. His brother, Alistair, was also employed for a time. Frank Bremner, an ex-lighthouse keeper,

Sjoglimt *on the slip at Askoy.*

Sjoglimt *in Bergen, ready for sea.*

Engineer Wilfie Bruce and skipper Alistair Goodlad.

Former HBP engineers, Jocob Bo and Inge Koltveit wave goodbye, March 1989.

At sea.

John Rognaldsen, Bressay, on a cage in Aiths Voe. John Goodlad *Douglas Scollay, Bressay.* *Elizabeth Scollay*

Feeding fish in Aithsvoe with a water cannon. *John Goodlad*

was employed regularly on a casual basis and after my time, became a full time employee.

Jamie Grunberg was a fulltime employee for several years. He was a good dependable worker and his diving skills were invaluable. Late one afternoon, I discovered something which required immediate attention and asked Jamie if he would come back in the evening to do the job. He considered for a moment before replying: "No, I'm not mentally prepared for that."

Needless to say I had to get mentally prepared to do the work myself.

Jamie would be surprised to hear how many times since then his expression has been used in our house.

Torbjørn Riise became a good stockman and a great support to me. During his first two weeks employment, I showed him what experience had taught me in salmon farming. He was as agile as a cat, with a surge of energy that I had lost somewhere along the way.

Bjarnhild and I were invited to a cocktail party at Gardie house on Boxing Day 1995. I was not happy at the prospect of Torbjørn going out on his own to feed the fish, but he was confident that he would manage fine. As a precaution I told him that he could contact me at Gardie in the event of a problem. The party was coming to life when John Scott asked me to come to the phone.

Not surprisingly, it was Torbjørn. The wind had by then increased to gale force and Torbjørn informed me that there was severe damage to a cage containing 10,000 salmon with a market value of £70,000. He had attempted to do first aid but was forced to give up. Luckily we had an empty cage complete with net on the site. I made contact with the skipper of the Norwegian Well Boat *Martin Sæle* who immediately came to the rescue. The fish were successfully pumped on board and then delivered into the empty cage. By seven pm we were home, the rescue operation complete.

Arriving at the time of depression within the white fish fleet, with decommissioning of boats and a downslide in shore employment, Salmon farming was a great boost to the local economy. In the early days of salmon farming some 50 Shetland owned companies were in operation.

A local Salmon Farmers Association was formed, which became invaluable to the industry. Meetings were held regularly and were well attended. We shared views and discussed regulations, and made decisions for the general wellbeing of the industry. It gave an opportunity to meet fellow fish farmers where friendships evolved and mutual problems discussed. The annual dinner dance was something to look forward to, creating the atmosphere of a large family.

The Scottish Salmon farmer's conference and exhibition was also a special yearly event. On the final night of the event, the dinner dance was a great opportunity to let the hair down and have some fun.

It was perhaps inevitable that this ideal situation of Shetland ownership would not last. Over-production of farmed salmon led to rock bottom prices, and for several years many farms were operating at a loss.

Bressay Salmon's survival was coupled to a number of factors. As Fulmar's agent, I was privileged to buy feed at discounted prices. An agreement of five months credit terms on feed helped the cash flow immensely, enabling us to grow the fish to a more profitable size. I got weekly pricelists from several different buyers and sold to the highest bidder. Our fish were of premium quality and were in demand. One buyer had some regular 'smoker' customers who asked specially, and were prepared to wait, for supplies from Bressay Salmon.

Bjarnhild did the book keeping and became an expert at credit control. I had learned much from the experience of others and always kept an ear to the ground. As Scottish agent for a Norwegian net manufacturer, I was in the fortunate position of meeting many fellow fish farmers.

A Norwegian Salmon farmer, whom I got to know, told me that he had achieved a growth rate of 2 kg fish by Christmas (45gr to 2 kg in 8 months).

"How on earth did you manage that?" I asked.

"It is quite simple" he said "but you need to have much patience. For the first three months of their sea life, you must feed the salmon three times a day. You must time the feeds to as near as possible 8 hours between, and then you must stand there, feeding slowly until they have eaten the last pellet. This should be 2% of the biomass per day."

I put his advice into practice, and it worked. For the first time we had 2 kg fish by Christmas. I must admit though that I spent many long hours, early and late, on the farm that summer, but it was worth the effort.

The practice today is that a 'well boat' collects live fish from the farms to be delivered live to the packing stations, lowering the temperature by refrigeration to 4.5°C. Automation had started creeping in towards the end of the century but, during my time, fish was slaughtered at the cages.

Sea water was added to the 1,000 litre bins, using many bags of ice to lower the temperature. It was labour intensive work where we employed casual labour (usually ferry men, during their free time). Peter Manson was a regular hand during his free time from the tugs at Sullom Voe. Peter was an ex-rigger and his skill with boats, handling anchors and rope splicing, was invaluable.

We had planned to harvest on a Thursday in mid-winter, but a storm put paid to the schedule. Hearing in the weather forecast that the wind would drop, I called Alistair at the Scalloway packing station.

"Can you pack our fish tomorrow?" I asked.

"Yes, provided that you have them here in Scalloway by 8 o'clock in the morning."

And so I contacted the crew, asking them to be at Heogan for a 2 30 am start. When I arrived at the pier, the boats engine was running, deck lights were blazing and the crew, all clad in oilskins, were ready for sea. They were, however, unusually quiet. To break the ice, I said.

"Well boys, I don't know whether to say good morning or goodnight."

Peter Manson cut in quickly: "You *could* say goodbye".

On 5th January 1993, in the teeth of a gale, disaster struck Shetland's Salmon Farming industry. The oil tanker *Braer* had passed Sumburgh Head, travelling in a westerly direction when her engines failed. She was driven ashore at Quendale, spewing thousands of tons of crude oil into the sea.

We had the VHF radio switched on and heard the conversation between two Norwegian oil supply boats. One was nearby and had offered assistance to the stricken tanker, but unbelievably, the offer was turned down. We heard the Norwegian skipper say: "Nu driver dem på land," (Now, they are drifting ashore).

Bjarnhild and I immediately jumped in our car to catch the ferry, and drove south. A distinct smell of oil filled the air. We could not see the stricken tanker from Sumburgh Head, but I took some photos of the huge waves breaking on the shore. The wind was so strong there that I could not stand upright.

The storm raged for several weeks. It must be the only time in memory that no adverse remark was made to a howling gale. The slogan was: "Let it blow, the waves will disperse the oil on the beaches."

Nevertheless, the loss to the industry was horrendous. Practically all the salmon on Shetlands west side were wiped out or had to be destroyed. The media had a field day flocking to Shetland like migrating birds. I was asked to take an Italian lady journalist out to our site. Holding up a salmon for the camera I commented.

"There's nothing wrong with these fish, they have not been affected by the oil spill."

"Oh you mustn't say that" she cut in.

Her only interest was to get a story. Some days later, we got a call from Sweden. Bjarnhild's brother in law had been surprised to see me on French TV, holding up a prime fish.

Tulloch Enterprises had arranged a seminar and a meal at the Shetland Hotel in conjunction with our Norwegian cage and net suppliers. All the Shetland farmers with their wives had been invited to attend. Just days before the planned event, crude oil was polluting Shetlands shoreline. The comment from Norway was: "You may as well cancel the event, no-one will come."

I called around for a reaction, and the result was that almost everyone wanted to attend. On the night, everyone was discussing the oil spill and its inevitable consequences, but the evening turned out to be a very successful event.

The Bressay car ferry *Leirna* was tied up for several days while the storm raged and the port authority pilot boat provided an emergency service. When our two Norwegian representatives arrived, they and two Norwegian media people made the crossing by the emergency service.

An addition to the Tulloch family was pending. Fiona and Rune made the emergency crossing in the nick of time for the arrival of Philip James, our youngest grandson.

At the fish farming dinner, a twist of fate that evening led to Tulloch Enterprises becoming agents for a Norwegian marina manufacturer. During the following years, we installed half of Shetland's 22 marinas.

By the turn of the century, huge changes were afoot within the industry. Many of the original small farms had either gone to the wall, or had been bought out by the handful of large companies that now own and control the industry.

In the year 2000, I sold my shares to the fellow directors and retired from salmon farming. The 12 years spent in the industry had been a great experience and something that I would not have missed.

Bressay Salmon's future was unfortunately short lived. Within two years the company, together with several medium sized farms in Shetland at the time went into receivership. Aiths Voe, however, continued to be used as a site for rearing halibut for some time through a new fish farming venture undertaken by Alistair and John Goodlad.

HEOGAN

17

THE 1990S AND A NEW MILLENNIUM

BY THE late 1980s Herring By-Products owned five fish meal and oil factories in the UK namely Fraserburgh, Bressay, Stornaway, Hull and Barra. HBP had invested heavily in modernising the Bressay, Fraserburgh and Barra factories. At Heogan alone, the estimated value of the factory in mid 1986 was £3.5m. The company had also invested in similar factories in America and in fresh water shrimp farming in Africa.

Helge Hovland was vice-chairman of the mother company. He had been the driving force behind the new investments. With his sudden death in the late 1980s, combined with Christian's death in 1989, the company went into decline.

The factory at Barra was the first to close, and 1990 saw the closure of the Heogan factory. Sadly, the factory at Fraserburgh was dismantled and is now gone without trace. The prosperous company which had traded successfully for fifty-five years had served the industry well.

All was not lost for Heogan however. In 1990, a new company Shetland Fish Products Ltd. (SFP) was formed to take over the business. Fifty per cent of the shares were taken up by United Fish Products of Aberdeen (UFP) – the Aberdeen fish Meal Company. The remaining 50% was taken up by a consortium of local fishing and marine organisations and companies.

They were: Seafood Shetland 16.7%, the Shetland PO 11.1%, Shetland Catch 11.1%, and Lerwick Port Authority (LPA) 11.1%. Shetland Norse had been an original shareholder but sold their shares to Seafood Shetland. For the first time there was a degree of local ownership of the Heogan factory.

Roger Donald's retirement, 1990, Bressay. From left: Johnny Smith, Sandy Lippe, Bert Henderson, Alistair Scollay, Mike Tippen (Manager), Ronald Henderson, Roger Donald, Robert Harkness, John McPhee, John Bremner; Sverre Riise, Geir Ola Riise, Laurence Manson, Carlos Riise, Andrew Paton, Edwin Gifford, Stuart Hunter; Ewan Anderson, Pat Tulloch, Keith Anderson, Elizabeth Scollay Lillian Anderson.

148

The new company acquired the factory and site at a fraction of its value, allowing them to make considerable investment. Most important was building two new deep water piers to cater for the ever increasing size of fishing vessels. A fish pump, new conveyor system and additional fish storage were all part of the investment.

The Shanty *at the end of her days.*   George Birnie

Inside the factory, a new boiler, drier and evaporation plant were installed. More stringent measures were applied to effluent discharge, to meet increasing demands by SEPA. The whole site got a facelift under the supervision of Managing Director Helge Korsager, and plans for expansion were afoot. Massive foreign fishing boats were attracted by the new facilities and intakes escalated, reaching a record breaking peak of 63,440 tonnes in 1995/96, a combination of mostly blue whiting and Atlanto-Scandian herring.

Johnny Smith and the fish pump.   Rune Tulloch

Helge Korsager, a Dane, was born into the fish meal industry – his father had been Manager of a fishmeal plant and Helge had worked in fish meal plants in Denmark before moving to Aberdeen to manage the UFP plant there. After SFP had been set up he took over the management of the operation at Heogan in addition to managing the Aberdeen factory.

In the early years of the 21st century the factory was thriving, but trouble lay ahead. UFP of Aberdeen had been bought over by IAWS – a large feed company based in the Republic of Ireland. IAWS therefore became a 50% shareholder in the Heogan factory. After a few years IAWS began to express doubts about the long term viability of Heogan. Supplies of fish were becoming scarcer as the blue whiting quota was reduced. Losses were being made and the future again looked bleak. IAWS had replaced Helge Korsager as Managing Director, a decision that did not bode well for the future. Helge had been a successful MD during the SFP years and had overseen an increase in production levels and a major capital investment program.

Adding to the uncertainty was a proposal by an Icelandic company to build a fish meal and oil factory at Sullom Voe. Unbelievably, Shetland

Altaire. *SFP*

Icelandic boat discharging at Heogan. *SFP*

Icelandic and Bressay salmon boats.   *SFP*

Sand eels.   *SFP*

Icelandic boat Huginn. *SFP*

Norwegian boat M-Fjord. *SFP*

Loading arm in action.   *SFP*

Loading a meal boat at the new pier.   *SFP*

Islands Council was prepared to back them to the tune of £5million in the provision of a new pier. With the eventual crash in blue whiting quotas nothing came of this proposal.

By 2008, Heogan was again in a crisis situation when IAWS eventually took a decision that it wanted to close the factory. The Shetland shareholders did not agree. As the Shetland shareholders held 50% of the shares there was deadlock. One obvious solution was for the Shetland shareholders to buy out their IAWS partners.

After much negotiation, two of the Shetland shareholders, Lerwick Port Authority and Shetland Catch bought the IAWS 50% shareholding. This meant that for the first time in its history, Heogan was 100% Shetland owned.

Following this buy out, LPA and Shetland Catch shareholding increased to 36.1% each, while Shetland Seafood and the Shetland PO retained their original 16.7% and 11.1% respectively. The deal was concluded in early 2009. Although the shareholding had substantially changed, it was decided to keep the company name of SFP – Shetland Fish Products.

A new board of Directors was appointed with the chairman of Shetland Catch, John Goodlad, becoming chairman of the new company. John's connection with Heogan went back a long way. As a student he had worked there loading meal boats during his summer holidays, The other Directors were Sandra Laurenson from Lerwick Port Authority, Ruth Henderson from Seafood Shetland and Brian Isbister from the Shetland PO.

John contacted Helge Korsager who was prepared to return to Heogan as MD. Brian Pottinger was Factory Manager and after a short time he also became a Director.

Brian Pottinger, the present day manager at Heogan, started a fishing career on board the Burra boat *Sunshine*. He got his skippers certificate and worked on various vessels both whitefish and pelagic, going from deckhand to skipper. After 22 years in the industry he sold the *Starina*, his last boat. He then went on to get an HNC in fisheries science and technology at the North Atlantic Fisheries College in Scalloway. In 2000 Brian started a new career at Heogan as administrator, then as production manager and in 2009 was promoted to manager and company director.

Shetlands fishing industry has changed almost beyond recognition since the 1950s. The drift net herring fleet was gradually phased out to be replaced by modern steel boats, complete with hydraulic power blocks and every modern device, greatly improving working conditions for fishermen.

With every available aid in fish finding devices, it became necessary to impose restrictions and new regulations to combat over-fishing. The disastrous exploitation of our herring stocks in the 1960s and 70s must not be forgotten. Nevertheless, the Common Fisheries Policy with separate quotas on individual species has not worked in favour of conservation; it has in part had the opposite effect. No fisherman can control which species will be caught in his net. Consequently, the protected species, cod for example, often go over the side, dead.

Dumping prime cod does nothing for conservation. The knock on effect is that more haddock, whiting and other species have to be caught in order to reach the total allowable quota. A blanket quota, including all species, would help to reduce the practice of dumping prime fish. A ruling that all fish caught must be landed should apply (as it does in Norway today) This would encourage fishermen to use legal mesh size nets, thereby reducing the tonnage of small fish caught, which today are simply dumped back into the sea. All rejected fish should be landed and go back into the food chain as fish meal.

Indiscriminate dumping of small fish has gone on for many years. One day in 1964 I saw an east coast fishing boat lying at the Heogan pier and, out of curiosity, went to investigate. The boat had its side decks full, and the crew were busy gutting and icing down the edible fish. All the small fish were being thrown over the side. I was shocked to see such waste and asked the skipper: "Can't you put that small fish up the conveyor belt instead of dumping them?"

"Oh we darena dee that," was the reply.

I have thought about that episode many times and of the adverse knock-on effects of unsound regulations. It is sad to see the downturn of

Pelagic boats at Symbister Harbour, 2005.

Shetland's white fish fleet. Boats have been decommissioned in the name of conservation. The whitefish fleet has declined from around 35 boats to the present day number of 23. The decline in Shetland, however, has been less than elsewhere, and we now have a very modern and efficient white fish fleet.

During the 1970s, a yearly conference of managers and engineers was arranged by the British Association of Fish Meal Manufacturers. The meetings were held at different locations each year and invariably included a visit to a fish meal factory. One year the conference was held in Denmark, where we visited five factories. I was very interested to see their fish bins, but was shocked to discover that their raw material consisted basically of immature fish of many species.

On enquiring what species they were processing, I got the same answer at each factory, 'Calypso' the Danish by-name for pout. The regulations allowed a by-catch of ten percent edible species in industrial landings. This ruling was strictly adhered to in the UK, but in Denmark 10% pout would have been nearer the mark. It was noted, however, that virtually no fish of edible size were to be seen.

We should ask: Was the Danish practice of 40 years ago, more wrong than the indiscriminate dumping of recent times? How many tons of valuable food has been dumped by our own fishermen in the name of conservation?

This book would not be complete without mentioning the important role played by women at Heogan, as office workers, lab and canteen assistants and cleaners. Special recognition should go to Marion Scollay who has kept the canteen and offices clean for some 22 years. She proved her talent with a camera when she went up in a helicopter to take this aerial view of the site.

What does the future hold for the factory at Heogan?

It would be a brave man who predicted anything to do with the fishing industry, but in order to look to the future we should reflect on the past. A factory has stood at Heogan for almost 130 years, serving as a vital link and aid to Shetland's fishing community. The industry can not survive without facilities to process offal and rejected fish. Gone are the days when it could simply be dumped back into the sea. The reduction plant at Heogan has gone through many crises situations, but it has survived, always adapting to meet the ever changing needs of the industry. Recent downturn in industrial fishing has once more led to a severe lack of supplies and it became necessary to change tactics once more.

Aerial view during the 1990s.   *Marion Scollay*

It has been rewarding to see some recovery during 2012 and to see so many trucks heading for Heogan during the summer months. The factory was again working round the clock for some weeks during the herring season, with the Bressay ferry running till 2am to cope with the extra traffic. Fish intakes for 12 months ending 31st August 2012 totalled some 14,000 tons offal, a record breaking year for offal. It surpasses the previous record of 1971, when 10,220 tons offal was processed. During that year, however, total fish intakes were 36,215 tons. In spite of recent difficulties, the prospects for Heogan probably look better than they have been for some time.

Hebbie Tulloch and Jamie Henry celebrate fifty years on from starting work at Heogan, 18ᵗʰ May, 2005.

In the first place SFP have recognised that the days of processing large tonnage of industrial catches are over. Instead it has focused on processing rejects and offal from the salmon packing plants and Shetland Catch. The processing operation has been geared up to deal with these supplies.

The potential to fillet more pelagic fish and salmon in Shetland factories would result in an increased volume at Heogan.

In the second place, The Heogan factory is in good shape having benefited from substantial investment and a good maintenance program during the past thirty years. The two new piers and sophisticated conveying system which gave such a boost during the 1990s are an asset, ready for use should the need arise. Now for the first time in its history, lack of facilities is no longer a problem at Heogan.

Finally, Heogan is now owned exclusively by Shetland interests. While the company still has to be viable to continue operating, the Shetland owners are far more likely to take a long term view of the future than outside owners would do.

What Bressay and the factory need more than anything else is provision of the promised and much debated fixed link. It beggars belief that EEC funding was allowed to be lost due to internal disagreement.

Fishing has always been uncertain, but Shetland needs a fish reduction plant. Since the 1880s this service has been provided at Heogan.

Now, some 130 years on, Heogan is still playing a crucial role in the modern Shetland fishing industry. Few businesses have had such a long history. With the new ownership structure and the changes made to the business, the future looks much brighter. There are good reasons for being confident that the Heogan factory will continue to operate well into its second century.

Staff reunion in 2010. From left – back row: John Paton, Johnny Smith, John Pottinger, Brian Pottinger, Adam Gifford, Dag Tulloch, Alistair Christie-Henry, Andrew Tulloch, Ewan Georgeson, Bruce Stickle, Gary Henderson, Richard Birnie, Ewan Anderson, Magnie Tulloch, Andrew Paton, Martin Hunter. Next row: Roy Tait, Jim Gruneberg, David Manson, George Williamson, Keith Anderson, Laurence Anderson, Bill Morris, Leonard Groat, Peter Tulloch, Rune Tulloch, Stewart Hunter, Sandy Lippe, Billy Clark, Grant Hunter, Peter Smith, Donald Manson, Charles Christie-Henry, Edwin Gifford, David Anderson, Ian Selbie. Next row: Jean Anderson, Marjory Hunter, Ray Tulloch, Lindis Tulloch, Magnie Ratter, Raymond Tulloch, Ian Nicolson, Clair Sutherland, Lawrence Manson, John Bremner, Harry Tulloch, John Kelsey. Front: Marion Scollay, Bjarnhild Tulloch, Hebbie Tulloch.
John Coutts

Gathering for the reunion at the Heogan canteen.   *Brian Pottinger*

Refreshments are served.   *Brian Pottinger*

Brian Pottinger and Hebbie   *Laurence Manson, Sandy Lippe and Hebbie*
Tulloch.   Brian Pottinger   *Tulloch, 2010.   Brian Pottinger*

John Coutts

The Tulloch family back at Heogan for the reunion in 2010. From left: Rune, Hebbie, Bjarnhild, Dag.
John Coutts

HBP DIRECTORS 1935 TO 1990

Sigfinn Bartz-Johannnessen
Coompany Founder

Christian Bartz-Johannnessen
Sigfinn's son – Chairman since 1945

Petter Bartz-Johannnessen
Sigfinn's grandson – Director

Ferdinand Meyer
Financial Advisor

George Reid
Director 1946; M.D. 1965-1981

Ian Hughes
Director 1963; M.D. 1981-1984

Helge Hovland
Vice-Chairman of the Board

Ken Maitland
M.D. 1984-1990

Gordon Wilson
Director 1966-1990

The author with the current SFP Directors, 4ᵗʰ December, 2012. Back: Helge Korsager,
Brian Isbister, Brian Pottinger. Front: Sandra Laurenson, John Goodlad, Hebbie
Tulloch. Missing from the photograph is Ruth Henderson.   *John Coutts*

OWNERS / SHAREHOLDERS

	Source of information	
1888 – 1889	Valuation role	Summerville & Co., Montrose
1892 – 1893	Manson's Almanac	The Highland Fish oil & Manure Co.
1897 – 1898	Valuation role	The Highland Fish oil & Manure Co.
1908 – 1935	Valuation role	The British Oil & Guano Co.
1935 – 1939	John Scott	Herring By-Products Ltd.
1939 – 1946	John Scott	Requisitioned by Ministry of Defence
1946 – 1990	Company records	Herring By-Products Ltd.
1990 – 2008	John Goodlad	Shetland Fish Products Ltd. (Shareholders: United Fish Products, Shetland PO, Shetland Catch and Seafood Shetland)

In 2009 there was a change of shareholders, but the name Shetland Fish Products was retained.

The new shareholders were:
Lerwick Port Authority, Shetland Catch
Shetland PO and Seafood Shetland

FACTORY MANAGERS

1893 –	James Mitchell
1908 –	J. Imrie
1909 –	W. Laird
1910 –	James MacDonald
1922 – 1939	Charles Johnston
1939 – 1946	Ministry of Defence
1946 –	Hilmar Onnerheim
1955	George Wills
1955 – 1957	Charlie Taylor (Fraserburgh)
1957 – 1964	Andrew White
1964 – 1986	James H. Tulloch
1986 – 1990	Mike Tippen
1993 – 1998	Alistair Stewart
1998 – 2009	Mike Swinburn
2009 –	Brian Pottinger

EMPLOYEES

THE following list of employees is compiled from available records and from memory where records are not available. Many students were employed during the 1970s and, unfortunately, the records have been lost for that period.

Where information is lacking I/L is inserted. The lists are in alphabetical order for each decade. Employees who have worked during different decades are listed in the first decade of their employment.

1950S

Name	Time Employed	Job Title
Laurence Anderson: Bressay	Mid 1950s &1967	Office
Robbie Anderson: Sullom	1950s	Handyman
Tammie Aitkin: Dunrossness	mid 1950s	Separators
Jamie Bairnson: Dunrossness	mid 1950s	Loft Man
John Bairnson: Dunrossness	mid 1950s	Pits
Willie Birnie: Bressay	1950s	Meal Store
Johnnie Dalziel: Bressay	mid 1950s	Drier Man
Willie Birnie: Bressay	1950s	Meal Store
Joe Campbell: Fraserburgh	mid 1950s	Foreman
Johnnie Dalziel: Bressay	mid 1950s	Drier Man
A Duncan: Shetland Mainland	mid 1950s	Spare Man
Geordie Eunson: Dunrossness	mid 1950s	Spare Man
Willie Flaws:Dunrossness	mid 1950s	Drier Man
Magnie Fraser: Bressay	1950s several years	Pits
Leonard Groat: Lerwick	the 1940s	I/L
Roald Hansen: Mossbank	1956-59	Separators / Launch Driver
James Christie-Henry: Bressay	May1955/1960, 1964/1973	Foreman/ Construction Leader
Angus Hoseason. Yell	mid 1950s	Spare Man
Jamie Jamison: Shetland Mainland	mid 1950s	Day Worker
Jackie Johnston: Dunrossness	mid 1950s	Separators
Willie Laurenson: Bressay	mid 1950s	Pits
Willie Leask: Bressay	mid 1950s	Pits
Dovie Linklater: Bressay	mid 1950s/1964	Meal Store
Hector Macdonald: Bressay	1950s-1965	Boatman
James Macdonald: Bressay	1950s-1965	Pier Man
Harald Manson: Bressay	1957 &1967	Pits

1950S — CONTINUED

Name	Time Employed	Job Title
Jamie Manson: Bressay	mid 1950s	Meal Store
Lowrie Manson: Bressay	mid 1950s	Pits
Peter Manson: Bressay	mid 1950s	Drier Man
Willie Manson: Bressay	mid 1950s-1960s	Pits
Willie Moar: Yell	mid 1950s	Loft Man
Bill Morgan: Lerwick	mid 1950s	Fireman
Andrew Mullay: Bigton	mid 1950s	I/L
Ewan Oddie: Yell	mid 1950s	Loft Man
Willie Priest:Yell	mid 1950s	Loft Man
Kenny Ramsay I/L	mid 1950s	I/L
Rasmie Reid: Culswick	1950s	Pits
Robbie Robertson: Brunthamersland	1950s	Meal Store
Peter Sandilands: Bressay	mid 1950s	Loft Man
Robbie Sinclair: Bressay	1950s	Drier Man
Geordie Smith: Levenwick	mid 1950s	Drier Man
J R Smith: Bressay	mid 1950s	Odd Job Man
Davie Strachan: Yell	mid 1950s	Loft Man
Ian Summers: Bressay	mid 1950s	Foreman
Charlie Taylor: Fraserburgh	1955/'56	Manager
Geordie Tulloch: Bressay	mid 1950s	Press Man
James H Tulloch: Bressay	1955	Factory Work
	1960	Foreman
	1964/'86	Manager
Ray Tulloch: Bressay	1957	General Duties
	1965-1966	Truck Driver
	1967	Foreman / Assistant Manager
	1975/1977	Joint Manager
Andrew G White: Bressay	1950s	Assistant Manager
	1957/1964	Manager
Davie White: Bressay	1930s & 1940s/1962	Oilman
Mary White: Bressay	1950s	Cook
John R Williamson: Yell	mid 1950s	Press Man
James Wiseman: Lerwick	1950s	Flitboat
Jamie Watt: Lerwick	1950s	Flitboat
(Mrs) Wilson: Lerwick	1950s	Assistant Cook
Geordie Yates: Bressay	1950s	Meal Store
Magnie Yates: Bressay	1950s	Boiler Man
H Young: Lerwick	1950s	Odd Jobs

1960s

Name	Time Employed	Job Title
Davy Anderson: Bressay	1969/'79	Boiler Man/Fitter
Maurice Anderson: Bressay	1968/'78 1978/'86	Office Assistant Manager
Robert Corkish: Lerwick	June/Aug1967	Meal Store
Michael Batty: Lerwick	Aug 1966	Meal Store
Ronald Birnie: Bressay	1960/'64	Separators
Winkie Birnie: Bressay	Aug1966	Meal Store
Tom Black: Bressay	1967	Meal Store
Barry Byrne: Bressay	Aug/Oct 1968	Meal Store
Andy Carter: Lerwick	April 1968	Plant Operator
Steve Chicken: I/L	Aug 1968	Meal Store
Alistair Christie-Henry: Bressay	Aug 1966	Meal Store
Charles Christie-Henry: Bressay	1968/70s	Meal Store Plant Operator/ Construction
Jimbo Clark: Bressay	Aug1967/78	Boatman
Robbie Cooper: I/L	Feb1966/'70s	Meal Store
Robert Corkish: Bressay	June- August 1963	Meal Store
James Craigie: Bressay	1968	Separators
James Cumming: Bressay	Jan1968/late1980s	Boatman/Canteen
James Deyell: Bressay	Sept1967/'70s	Construction
Roger Donald: Bressay	Feb1966/March'90	Separators/Foreman
Robbie Eunson: Bressay	June 1967/ 1970s	Construction
Alistair Gardner: Bressay	1967/70s	Storeman
Laurence Gifford: Bressay	May1964/74	Plant Operator/ Foreman
Willie Gordon: Bressay	June/Oct1967	Pits
John Gray: Lerwick	I/L	Fitter
James Grunberg: Bressay	June/Dec1968	Meal Store
James Hall: Lerwick	Aug 1966	Meal Store
C Henderson: Lerwick	Aug 1966	Meal Store
Graham Henderson: Bressay	1965'75	Truck Driver/Boatman
G.W Henderson: Lerwick	Aug 1966	I/L
Harry Hunter: Bressay	1967/'70s	Evaporators
Chris Jacobson: Bressay	Oct/Nov1968	Meal Store
J Laurenson: I/L	March/ June1963	I/L
Robbie Leask: Lerwick	March/ June 1963	I/L
Sandy Lippe: Fraserburgh	July1969/Oct'90	Engineering
W McDougal: Lerwick	Aug 1968	Meal Store
Jim McKay: Bressay	1967/75	Plant Operator/ Foreman
McKenzie: Lerwick	Aug 1968	Meal Store
A Manson: Lerwick	Aug 1968	Pits
Davie Manson: Quarff	1960s	Construction

1960S – CONTINUED

Name	Time Employed	Job Title
David Manson: Bressay	1967	Meal Store
Donald Manson: Bressay	March 1965/'69	Truck Driver
Tammie H Manson: Bressay	Feb1965/Oct'90	Plant Operator
M Mazzaschi: Lerwick	July 1968	Meal Store
Frank Moar: Lerwick	1968	Meal Store
J Moar: I/L	Aug 1966	Meal Store
Andy Newlands: Lerwick	Sept1968	Discharging Boats
Magnie Ratter: Bressay	May1968/'70s	Electrician
R Riordan: I/L	Aug/Oct 1966	Aug/Oct 1966
Robbie Robertson: Brunthamersland	Late 1960s	Dismantling Oil Store
Magnie Scollay: Lerwick	Dec 1968	Welder
Ian Selby: Lerwick	1960s/1970s	Engineering
John Simmons: Bressay	June 1967	Pits
Joe Smith: Bressay	June/Dec 1964	Pits/Meal Store
Stanly Smith: Bressay	Aug 1967	Meal Store
Ian Sinclair: Lerwick	Nov 1968/ I/L	Meal Store
Bertie Sutherland: Bressay	1968	Welding
Tommie Sorley: Lerwick	Aug 1966	Canteen
Charlie Stove: Bressay	(The 1930s,1 day in 1968)	Meal Store
Ian Stuart: I/L	Sept 1968	Meal Store
Geordie Sutherland: Bressay	Sept 1967& 1970s	Pits/Meal Store
I Sutherland: I/L	Aug 1966	Meal Store
Roy Tait: Lerwick:	Aug 1968	Meal Store
L Thompson: I/L	Aug 1966	Meal Store
G Thompson: I/L	Aug 1967	Meal Store
Andrew Tulloch: Bressay	1963/'67	Pits/Plant Operator
Angus Tulloch: Bressay	(1 day in 1968)	Meal Store
Harry Tulloch: Bressay	July1965/'70	Handyman/Construction
Harry S Tulloch: Bressay	April1968/'90 1990/'99	Plant Operator/Foreman Production Manager
James John Tulloch: Bressay	March 1966	Construction
Magnie Tulloch: Bressay	June1967/'70s	Cooker/ Press
Tom Tulloch: Bressay	Jan 1966	Meal Store
Willie Tulloch: Channerwick	July 1967	Meal Store
Davie Andrew White: Bressay	Late1960s	Pits
Attie Williamson: Lerwick	Aug 1966	Meal Store
George Williamson: Bressay	June1967/'69	Plant Operator
Magnie Williamson: Lerwick	Late 1960s	Welder
Frank Wiseman: Lerwick	Aug 1968	Meal Store
Teddy Wiseman: Lerwick	Sept1968	Discharging Boats/ Truck Driver
Charlie Williamson: Lerwick	Late 1960s	Engineering

1970S

Name	Time Employed	Job Title
Percy Agutter: Lerwick	1970s/'82	Evaporators
Joe Agnew: Bressay	Jan1978/Nov'85	Plant Operator
George Birnie: Bressay	1970s	Meal Store
Billy Clark: Bressay	1972/'75	Boatman
Johnnie Clark: Bressay	1970s/'80s	Canteen
Peter Dempster: Student	1970s	Meal Store
Ted Diamond: Tresta	1970s	Meal Store
Adam Gifford: Bressay	1973/75	Meal Store/Driers
Eric Fillmore: Bressay	The 1970s	Mechanic/Boiler Man
Ronald Henderson: Bressay	1970s/'80s	Pits
Colin Hendry: Lerwick	1970s	Electrician
Tommy Hughson: Bressay	1973/74	Meal Store
Martin Hunter: Tresta	early 1970s	Welder
Angus McKechnie: Bressay	1970s	Crain Driver
James Leask: Lerwick	I/L	Truck Driver
Davie MacGilvary: Scottish	1970s	Meal Store
Ian Nicholson: Tresta	1970s	Engineering
Tim Parkinson: Student	1970s	Meal Store
Andrew Paton: Lerwick	from the 1980s	Electrician
G.J. Peterson: Lerwick	Feb/July 1983	Meal Store
Geordie Petrie: Bressay	1970s	Construction
Jan Riise: Bressay	1972	Welder
Leonard Scollay: Bressay	1970s	Boatman
Jim Shepherd: Cumnock	1970s	Engineer
Bruce Stickle: Lerwick:	1970s for 9 Years	Plant Operator
Frank Sinclair: Lerwick	1970s	Meal Store
James Smith: Bressay	1977/'82	Plant Operator
Peter Smith: Lerwick	1970s	Electrician
Robin Strachan: Bressay	Sept1971/'75 & Aug'87/'88	Evaporators
Lollie Sutherland: Bressay	June1970/Sept'82	Pits/Pier Man
Clair Sutherland: Bressay	June1970/ May'76	Meal Store
Brian Taylor: Fraserburgh	1970s	Meal Store
Rory Taylor: Inverness	1970s	Meal Store
Dag Tulloch: Bressay	1974/'75	Meal Store
Lindis Tulloch: Bressay	July1979/Aug'86	Office
Robert Tulloch: Bressay	1971	Meal Store
Rune Tulloch: Bressay	1974 /'84 1990/'93	Engineering Engineering Manager
Jonathan Wills: Bressay	Early 1970s	Meal Store
Angus Wood: Bressay	Early 1970s	Meal Store
Arthur Wylie: Bressay	Nov1977/'84	Meal Store

1980s

Name	Time Employed	Job Title
A.E Anderson: I/L	1982	Meal Store
Ewan Anderson: Bressay	Feb1986/Oct 1990	Fitter
Jean Anderson: Bressay	April 1986/March 1986	Canteen
Keith Anderson: Bressay	April 1988/Oct 1990	Meal Store
Winkie Birnie: Bressay	March/ May1983	Meal Store
Robert Bishop: I/L	April/Sept 1982	Canteen
Robert Bishop: I/L	1985	Meal Store
S. Borthwick : I/L	June 1989 (five days)	I/L
John Bremner: Bressay	1989/'90 & 2001/2011	Plant Operator
M.F Campbell: Lossiemouth	March 1984/May 1985	Meal Store
Johnnie Clark: Bressay	1980s	Canteen
I.J Craigen: I/L	May/Aug 1983	I/L
Neil Donald: Bressay	1982	Engineering
G.F Dinning: Co Durham	April 1982	Meal Store
R.M Falconer: Lerwick	April 1985/ I/L	I/L
M.J Fraser: I/L	Aug/Sept 1988	Aug/Sept 1988
R Fraser: I/L	Aug/Oct 1988	I/L
D.O.M Gander: Vidlin	Feb/March 1983	Meal Store
A Garnett: Derbyshire	Oct 1984 (three weeks)	I/L
Edwin Gifford: Bressay	Aug 1989/Oct 1990	Plant Operator
M.W Gray: I/L	April 1984/ Sept 1985	I/L
Kenny Groat : Bressay	Dec1988/April'89	Plant Engineer
K Grunneberg: Hamnavoe	May 1987/April'88 & March/June 1989	Plant Operator
Bert Henderson: Bressay	July1981/Oct 1990	Canteen
Ronald Henderson: Bressay	March1982/Oct'90	Pits
Marjorie Hunter: Bressay	April/Sept 1982	Canteen
Stuart Hunter: Bressay	March 1981/Aug'90	Plant Operator
P Huntley: I/L	July 1989/ March'90	Plant Operator
W Ligget: I/L	March/June 1989	Plant Operator
L.S Irvine : I/L	May/Aug 1983	Plant Operator
Brian Laird: Lerwick	April/Aug 1986	Plant Operator
R Johnston: I/L	March 1987/April'89	Plant Operator
M Kent: I/L	April/Dec 1987	Plant Operator
John McPhee: Lerwick	July 1989/Oct'90	Plant Operator/ Foreman
Mary Mackechnie: Bressay	1983 &'85	Canteen
Frank McLean: West Lothian	April 1983/April'84	Welder
Laurence Manson: Bressay	March 1981 to date	Plant Operator / Boiler Man/ Plant Engineer

1980S – CONTINUED

Name	Time Employed	Job Title
George Mustard: Lerwick	June1982/July'83	Meal Store
Liza Ann Mustard Lerwick	June1982/July'83	Canteen
J.G Paterson : I/L	Feb/June 1983	Plant Operator
Ivor Pottenger: Hamnavoe	March/April 1983	Plant Operator
Michail Reddings: I/L	April/July 1986	Plant Operator
Carlos Riise: Bressay	June 1985/Oct'90	Plant Operator
Geir Olav Riise: Bressay	Feb1988/Oct'90	Plant Operator
Jan Robert Riise: Bressay	summer-season 1983/84/85	Painter/Plant Operator
Rangnar Riise: Bressay	July1989/March'90	Plant Operator
Sverre Riise: Bressay	March 1987/Jan'90	Plant Operator
Ingrid Ryder: Bressay	July/Jan 1987	Office
Alistair Scollay: Bressay	May1989/Oct'90	Plant Operator
Douglas Scollay: Bressay	June1980/May'84	Engineering
A Smith: I/L	April/Sept 1985	I/L
Alan Smith: Bressay	1983 (one day)	Odd Jobs
Johnnie Smith: Bressay	March1982 (periodic) to date	Plant Operator
Alistair Stuart: Ollaberry	June/Oct 1984 &1993/1998	Plant Operator Manager
Roy Tait: Lerwick	Early 1980s	Meal Store
F Tomlison: I/L	Aug 1986'July'89	Plant Operator
Peter Tulloch: Lerwick	Jan 1988/April'90	Plant Operator
T.H Tulloch: Lerwick	March/Oct 1984	Plant Operator
Raymond Tulloch: Bressay	July1981/ Sept'82 & June'85 / Sept'85	Engineering
R Watkins: Caravan Heogan	April 1986/'Jan89	Plant Operator
Peter Watson: Bressay	Aug 1983 (three weeks)	Meal Store
Steve Woo: I/L	1982	Meal Store
P.T Wentworth: I/L	May/July 1988	Meal Store
Stanley Wood: Tingwall	1982	Engineering

1990S — ONWARDS

Name	Time Employed	Job Title
Richard Birnie: Bressay	April/July 1990	Plant Operator
Serges Bondarevs Bressay	2004	Plant Operator
Dominique Bouchet: Bressay	2005	Plant Operator
Laurent Bromberg: Bressay	2004/05	Plant Operator
J Cheyne. : Lerwick	April/Aug 1990	Plant Operator
Njal Christie- Henry Bressay	2005	Plant Operator
Andy Dalziel: Bressay	1990s	Plant Operator
Keith Darlington: Bressay	1990s	Plant Operator/ Foreman
Michael Fielding: Virkie	1990s	Plant Operator
Ewan Georgeson: West Side	1996	Engineering Manager
Andy Goodman: Lerwick	2005	Plant Operator
Dougie Graham: Bressay	1998/2008	Plant Operator
Robert Harknes: Bressay	Feb/Nov 1990	Plant Operator
Marc Henry: Lerwick	2005	Plant Operator
Ross Hornal: Lerwick	2005	Plant Operator
Colin Hough Lerwick	2002	Plant Operator
Bryan Law: Bressay	2002/ 2007	Plant Operator
Basil Leask: Bressay	1991/'99	Office Manager
Scott Macintosh: Lerwick	2005	Plant Operator
P.Mcphee: Lerwick	April/Aug 1990	Plant Operator
Bill Morris: Bressay	late1990s	Plant Operator
Andrejs Mosurs: Scalloway	2005	Plant Operator
Marion Scollay: Bressay	May1991/date	Cleaning Office & Canteen
Tristan Sinclair: Bressay	2005	Plant Operator
Bob Smith: Bressay	April 2002/.2003	Plant Operator
Mick Swinburn: Lerwick	Sept 1995/98 1998/1999	Engineering Manager Manager
Denis Zalekesin: Bressay	Sept 2004	Plant Operator
Shane Winson: Lerwick	2005	Plant Operator

PRESENT EMPLOYEES

Name	Date Started	Job Title
Brian Pottinger: Lerwick	13 03 00	Manager
Gary Henderson: Whitness	19 08 03	Engineering Manager
Laurence Manson: Bressay	28 02 91	Plant Engineer
Frank Lawton: Whitness	19 12 94	Plant Operator
John Pottinger: Walls	14 10 03	Electrician
John Kelsey: Lerwick	22.08.94	Plant Operator
Marion Scollay	May 1991	Cleaner
Johnny Smith: Bressay	11.11.02	Plant Operator
Michael Millar: Scalloway	I/L	Plant Operator
Bruce Williamson: Lerwick	I/L	Plant Operator
Stephen Johnson: Lerwick	I/L	Plant Operator

FISH RECEIPTS AND
CHANGING SPECIES AT HEOGAN

DURING the early years, only herring offal was processed. The installation of second-hand plant from Norway in 1946 made it possible to process herring for the first time. During the late 1940s and 1950s, the drift net fleet fished herring exclusively for the factory during the month of May.

Production records prior to 1962 no longer exist. What is known is that maximum throughput, prior to the installation of new plant, was about 1⎯ tons in 24 hours. Therefore during the 1950s when the duration of the herring season was May till September, the factories capacity would have been about 18,000 tons for the season. Perhaps 60% of the potential would be a fair guess, equating to some 10,800 tons.

In 1957 whitefish offal became available, resulting in the factory operating 12 months of the year. Dog fish offal and crab shells were added to the menu and even seal carcases (on one occasion only). Surplus whitefish were turned into fishmeal when there was no alternative outlet, even to the extreme when the fleet fished for prime, edible fish to be landed at Heogan.

Here is a graph of supplies and detailed records of receipts for individual species starting in 1962, which I have retained for interest.

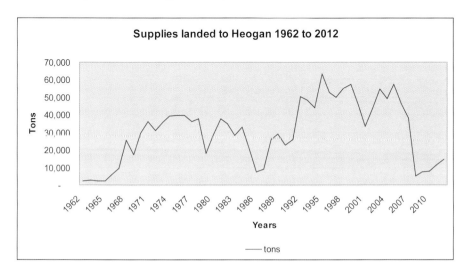

Fish Intakes 1962/1986

Year	Pout	Landing	Herring	Mackerel	Sprats	Blue Whiting	Sand Eel	White Fish	White Fish Offal	Herring Offal	Total
1962		Local	128						723	1,428	2,279
1963		Local	550						1,115	1,052	2,917
1964		Local	594						1,760	653	2,413
1965		Local	1,213						662	389	2,264
1966		Local	1,738		1,700				1,944	507	5,889
1967		Local	794		714				2,261	425	9,267
		Foreign	5,073								
1968	77	Local	561		44				1,948	515	23,594
	9,419	Foreign	11,035								
1969	233	Local	1,885		124				2,180	536	17,134
	3,340	Foreign	8,826								
1970	1,071	Local	6,429		33				4,849	701	29,635
	6,778	Foreign	9,771								
1971	169	Local	13,610		56				9,618	602	36,215
	5,886	Foreign	6,137		154						
1972	1,012	Local	8,010		334				4,132	625	31,117
	10,616	Foreign	6,384								
1973	6,907	Local	6,933		1,428				3,923	649	35,859
	10,626	Foreign	5,391								
1974	18,219	Local	3,272	1,168	172		7,662		3,712	648	39,394
	2,473	Foreign	428	920	472		246				
1975	14,009	Local	1,393	202	212		12,690		4,249	440	39,602
	4,050	Foreign	93	251	1,489		230	291			

Year											
1976	Local	11,074	84	851	865	93	18,718	73	4,840	484	39,806
	Foreign	2,038		64	607		9				
1977	Local	4,099	3	2,150	2,325		21986	102	4,959	168	36,187
	Foreign	292		100							
1978	Local	5,359		300	875		27,510	12	2,989		37,580
	Foreign	530									
1979	Local	2,872		443	247		12,815	8	1,253		18,214
	Foreign	245		239							
1980	Local	593		2,298		2649	22,283	105	735		28,666
1981	Local	825					36,196				37,752
	Foreign		731								
1982	Local	20					35,016				35,036
	Foreign										
1983	Local		79				28,251				28,330
1984		2,029	2,642	756			25,918				32,840
		1,437									
1985	Local		6,748	2,289			10,834				19,871
1986	Local		744				6,114				7,602
1987	Local		2,042	438			5,343		12		7835

Total intakes for the following years were:

1988 – 26,000 tons; 1989 – 29,000 tons; 1990 – 23,000 tons; 1991 – 26,000 tons

Year	Herring	Mackerel	Blue Whiting	Capelin	Horse Mackerel	Sand Eel	Shetland Sand Eel	Norway Pout	Ot2	White Offal	Oily Offal	Total
1992/93	1717	3873	21,262	4708	1532	2943	0	1091	1321	3940	8128	50,514
1993/94	1401	525	20437	776	3524	8949	0	132	1093	3973	7414	48,223
1994/95	12,626	138	16,141	0	741	5157	0	189	542	3229	5424	44,186
1995/96	21,708	1685	16,379	863	284	8728	0	95	2036	4857	6804	63,440
1996/97	6151	0	18,323	1769	0	14,081	0	470	291	5173	6384	52,642
1997/98	3394	123	23,097	1349	0	8169	2694	371	55	5102	5733	50,087
1998/99	914	10	34,074	0	0	2617	4776	832	32	4966	6909	55,132
1999/2000	5144	82	26,544	0	0	5241	5788	0	106	1733	12,898	57,536
2000/01	495	0	27,194	2107	0	295	1294	0	0	926	13,411	45,722
2001/02	0	0	16,778	0	0	1617	360	0	0	772	13,890	33,417
2002/03	0	0	29,129	0	0	0	543	0	0	850	13,028	43,551
2003/04	498	0	37,767	0	0	566	65	0	0	477	15,105	54,478
2004/05	0	0	31,796	0	0	0	0	0	0	210	17,313	49,319
2005/06	101	0	24,775	0	0	0	0	0	0	196	22,832	47,903
2006/07	2625	0	30,521	0	0	0	0	277	0	180	12,645	46,249
2007/08	0	0	34,962	0	0	0	0	0	0	158	2832	37,952
2008/09	0	0	229	0	0	0	0	0	0	100	4837	5166
2009/10	0	0	1017	0	0	0	0	0	0	198	6224	7439
2010/11	0	0	0	0	0	0	0	294	0	258	7335	7887
2011/12	0	0	0	0	0	0	0	0	0	236	11,139	11,375